Holiness and Mission

Learning from the Early Church about Mission in the City

Morna Hooker and
Frances Young

scm press

© Morna Hooker and Frances Young 2010
Appendix © Roger Cotterrell 2010

Published in 2010 by SCM Press
Editorial office
13–17 Long Lane,
London, EC1A 9PN, UK

SCM Press is an imprint of Hymns Ancient and Modern Ltd
(a registered charity)
13 A Hellesdon Park Road
Norwich NR6 5DR, UK
www.scm-canterburypress.co.uk

Except where otherwise indicated, Bible quotations are either the authors'
own translation or are from the New Revised Standard Version of the Bible,
copyright 1989 by the Division of Christian Education of the National Council
of the Churches of Christ in the USA. Used by permission. All rights reserved.

Other scripture quotations are the authors' own translations.

British Library Cataloguing in Publication data

A catalogue record for this book is available
from the British Library

978-0-334-04381-2

Originated by The Manila Typesetting Company
Printed and bound by
CPI Antony Rowe, Chippenham, SN14 6LH

Contents

Preface

It is our hope that those people presently exercised about mission and the spread of the Christian gospel in our post-Christian society will find these studies of scripture and the early Church pertinent to their thinking. Although the main chapters focus on biblical and historical material, the final chapter makes some attempt to draw out conclusions for the Church today; but the work is offered in the spirit of provoking reflection on potential parallels rather than offering ready-made answers. Insofar as we have any expertise, it lies in providing insight into the early history and the fundamental texts of the Christian faith, but in selecting the material we have been influenced by an awareness of the contemporary context within which the Church now needs to pursue its calling to participate in God's mission.

In particular we focus on mission in the city. This is because the book began life as the Hugh Price Hughes lectures in 2010, delivered at Hinde Street Methodist Church in London during Lent, the context being the celebration of 250 years of Methodism in the West End and 200 years on the present site. The subject of 'mission' and in particular 'mission in the city' commended itself because Hinde Street is now the headquarters of the West London Mission Circuit, inheriting the work of notable leaders such as Hugh Price Hughes and Donald Soper at Kingsway Hall. We are pleased that the enthusiastic response to the lectures led Roger Cotterrell (a member of Hinde Street Church, Anniversary Professor of Legal Theory at Queen Mary University of London and a Fellow of the British Academy) to compile an appendix gathering together diverse voices from the audience, who spoke out of the experience of trying to live as Christians in the urban environment. However, the theological and practical issues we discuss are hopefully of far wider relevance.

Yet that original context is important, not least because it was the invitation to the two of us from Hinde Street which occasioned our first, much appreciated opportunity to collaborate with one another. We have enjoyed working together, and we hope that our readers will discern something of the interest generated by this project.

Morna Hooker and Frances Young
April 2010

Introduction

In his book, on *Cities and People*, the architectural historian Mark Girouard begins by referring to big cities as romantic places 'in the sense in which William Morris used the word: "By romantic I mean looking as if something was going on".[1] He goes on to write about the way in which the roar and throb of a great city can be exciting or frightening. 'The rumble seems to become the inhuman sound of a mill which is remorselessly chewing up human beings.' But getting to know a city dissolves this 'impersonality', as one 'begins to distinguish the endless elements of which it is made up, different societies, different groups, different races, different religions, different family nexuses . . . all of which are constantly overlapping and interacting'. It is access to some of these groups and their interactions which 'makes human life endurable or enjoyable', he suggests.

City contexts of that kind were the locations in which Christianity spread, and what holds together the chapters of this book is a search for the kind of thing it has meant to embody the gospel and engage in mission in such places. In the first two chapters, Morna Hooker mines the biblical material for insight into the fundamental call and commission of the apostles, focusing first on the charge to 'Be holy as I am holy', what this implied for Israel and how it informed the apostolic mission to follow Jesus in doing the words and works of God. She then explores the adverse image of the city found in much of the biblical material, cities often figuring as places of oppression and injustice, and shows how Jesus and his followers presented a challenge to cities like Jerusalem and Rome. Yet in Acts these cities are identified as strategic centres, and cities facilitated the spread of the gospel. Rome appears as a force for good, as well as being the evil Babylon of the book of Revelation; and the climax of the Bible is in fact a vision of the New Jerusalem. The call is to embody the gospel whatever the cost, and being holy involves not just separation from the world or individual salvation but active presence engaging with the world's needs and problems. This is to imitate Emmanuel, God with us.

Chapters 3 and 4, by Frances Young, present some findings from historical research into the way Christianity actually spread in about the first five centuries of its existence – in the earliest period, before it had any official status and when it was subject to sporadic persecution and functioned as a somewhat anomalous minority group in the cities of the Roman Empire, and after the conversion of the Emperor Constantine, when the Church found itself patronized by state power and increasingly had to adapt to fulfil the functions in society expected of a religion. Her presentation of the history implies some potential parallels with the Church's current ambiguous position in post-Christian urban societies, hints at the possibility that when Constantine identified God's mission with his mission and the attempt was made to Christianize society as a whole some of the most fundamental aspects of the Christian gospel were compromised, and suggests implicitly that we might do better to learn how to embody the gospel in city environments from the Church of the pre-Constantinian period. Within the context of Roman cities, Christian groups looked most like a school presenting a new kind of philosophy, but people seem to have been attracted by belonging to a community, by support offered, both material and spiritual, and by the lived ethic of love, love of neighbour, stranger and even enemy. This would suggest that it is through belonging to open, overlapping networks that people can both discover and begin to embody the gospel in the 'rumble' and 'impersonality' of the soulless city.

So what about preaching the gospel? The legacy of the eighteenth-century Evangelical movement, together with the missionary expansion of the nineteenth century, means that mission is most often associated with evangelizing and conversion, with bringing people to faith and teaching them the truth. Many would feel that what is needed is a renewed sense of the apostolic commission to proclaim the Good News, especially in the context of the West, where Christianity seems to be on the retreat, routed by the forces of secularization and pluralism. But renewal and reformation often emerge from a return to origins and fundamental principles. In the final chapter, each of the contributors presents some reflections on the implications of the earlier chapters for mission today, briefly considering models and methods of mission, together with issues about truth questions, dogma and doctrine, proselytizing and other faiths. Such themes are taken up also in the Appendix, where contributions from the original audience are given voice. Inevitably only the surface is scratched, but there is common ground in the insistence that it is only by knowing God's love through hearing the gospel, and experiencing it through participation in loving communities, that people can be empowered to embody that love in lives lived for the sake for others.

Note

1. Mark Girouard, *Cities and People*, London: Guild Publishing, 1985, p. v.

Be Holy as I am Holy

MORNA HOOKER

You may perhaps have been puzzled by the title of this book, and found yourself wondering what holiness and mission have in common. Holiness we associate with personal sanctity, and we symbolize it with haloes, suggesting that saints are separated from the rest of us – often, indeed, withdrawing from the world altogether. Mission, on the other hand, means going out *into* the world – getting involved with all its activities. Why, then, begin a study of mission by talking about holiness?

The answer is: because it is with the idea of holiness that the Old Testament begins its awareness of Israel's mission to the world, and if we are to understand our own mission as Christians, then that is where we, too, must begin.

Israel's call to be holy

'Be holy as I am holy.' What does the Old Testament mean by holiness? The instinct that led us to suppose that saints are *separated* from others was correct, since to be holy originally meant, simply, to be separated, set apart. Holiness, first and foremost, was what differentiated God from men and women. Nevertheless, in summoning Israel to be his people, God demanded that they should share his 'otherness'. They must 'consecrate' themselves to him – make themselves holy, separate from other nations. We are not, however, talking about individuals, but about Israel, the whole nation. As John Wesley aptly expressed it, centuries later, biblical holiness is essentially *social* holiness: it concerns the whole community.[1] The demand is set out in Leviticus 11.44–45:

> I am the LORD your God; consecrate yourselves therefore, and be holy, for I am holy . . . For I am the LORD who brought you up

4

from the land of Egypt, to be your God; you shall be holy, for I am holy.[2]

You will notice that what God demands is based on what God has already done – on what the theologians term 'prevenient grace'. Yahweh has graciously chosen Israel as his special people, and her holiness depends on her relationship with him. She is to be holy as he is holy, to be *like* him. Holiness means living according to the revealed character of God. In Leviticus, 'being holy' is defined mainly in cultic terms. Israel is separated from other nations by rules about cleanliness. Later, however, the prophets interpreted holiness in what we would call ethical terms. God is 'the Holy One of Israel', and to speak of his holiness is to speak, in effect, of what he is. Since he himself is compassionate and just, what he requires of his people is, above all, justice and compassion for others. Those who are his people acknowledge Yahweh alone as God, and reflect his character as a righteous and loving God.

But *why* was Israel chosen as God's people? What was the *purpose* of her call? There are two kinds of answer. The first concentrates on the relationship between God and Israel. She is the recipient of his grace, and must therefore serve him by her worship and in her manner of life. Although this answer rightly sees that God's holiness demands purity on the part of his worshippers, and can lead to devotion and piety, it can also result in a community that is turned in upon itself and excludes outsiders. It takes the idea of separation from outsiders so seriously that it cuts them off. 'Be holy' is understood to mean 'Keep aloof'. According to Deuteronomy, when Israel entered the Promised Land, God drove out the nations already there, and instructed his people to exterminate those who were delivered into their hands. They must not intermarry with other nations, lest they draw them away from serving Yahweh, their God. They must pull down their altars and burn their idols, since they, Israel, were 'a people holy to the Lord' (Deuteronomy 7.1–6).

We see a later example of this attitude in the exclusive policy adopted by Nehemiah and Ezra, who rigorously separated their community from other nations: they were God's people – they alone – and they were concerned to keep their community pure. Later still, the members of the Dead Sea community at Qumran seem to

5

have had a similar understanding of the meaning of holiness, since they endeavoured to keep themselves separate from anyone who was unholy.[3] This was how the Pharisees – the name means 'the separated ones' – understood holiness, and how Paul had understood it before he became a Christian.[4] One can depict this response diagramatically, by means of a straight line joining two dots. God has called us, his people, to be holy, but God's grace apparently stops here, with us, the lucky recipients. The relationship between God and his people is seen as an exclusive one.

The alternative approach understood God's purpose in choosing the Jews as extending *beyond* Israel to the other nations. Certainly God had separated them from other nations – but it was for a purpose, and this purpose, paradoxically, *involved* the other nations. This time, the relationship is triangular, involving God, Israel and the Gentiles, so our diagram now must be of a triangle instead of a straight line. It is adumbrated already in the call of Abraham, who is chosen by God to be the ancestor of a great nation. Nevertheless, God's covenant with him includes the promise that he will be the source of blessing to *all* the nations of the earth.[5]

But it is the prophets who spell out the implications of what it meant to be God's holy people – in particular the prophet who wrote some of the later chapters of Isaiah. He understood God's call of Israel to be his people as a call to reveal him to the other nations. The basis of his understanding of Israel's role was his conviction that Yahweh, the God of Israel, was the only true God, and the gods worshipped by other nations did not in fact exist. If this God – the Holy One of Israel[6] – was the God of all the earth and all its peoples, should not they, too, be taught about him, and should they not worship and serve him? Israel's task was to be a witness to God's power and love – to be 'a light to the nations' (Isaiah 42.6) – since God's purpose was that his salvation should 'reach to the end of the earth' (Isaiah 49.6). Even earlier, another prophet had prophesied that the day would come when all the nations would flock to Jerusalem to worship God and learn his ways.[7] This idea was picked up by yet another prophet, who declared that on that day,

the foreigners who join themselves to the LORD,
    to minister to him, to love the name of the LORD,
    and to be his servants . . .

these I will bring to my holy mountain,
    and make them joyful in my house of prayer . . .
for my house shall be called a house of prayer
    for all peoples.

(Isaiah 56.6–7)

The prophet who spoke these words believed that God had chosen Israel as his people, and that her role was to reveal his glory to other nations.[8]

In what sense, then, is Israel a light to the nations? What form does her mission take? Another prophet who shared this vision of Israel's call wrote the book of Jonah, a story that symbolizes Israel's mission to other nations – and her reluctance to undertake the task given her. The prophet Jonah, after initially *refusing* God's commission, and taking flight, is depicted as finally obeying God's summons to go to Nineveh, where he proclaims the message entrusted to him – a message of coming judgement. When his words are effective, the people of Nineveh are – to Jonah's great annoyance – saved.

Usually, however, the witness seems to be in *deed* rather than word. Isaiah 42 speaks of God's Servant, who is probably to be identified with Israel, but if not, then the Servant is certainly the representative of Israel. The prophet describes how God's Servant will establish justice on the earth. God has called him and given him

. . . as a covenant to the people,
    a light to the nations,
        to open the eyes that are blind,
to bring out the prisoners from the dungeon,
    from the prison those who sit in darkness.

(Isaiah 42.6–7)

On Sinai, God had called Israel to be his people and made a covenant with her. Now, Israel is herself a covenant – the means of binding together God and the nations of the world. Israel herself had been brought out of darkness and slavery in Egypt, and her task now is to assist in doing for others what has been done for her: to open blind eyes, release prisoners, and establish justice on the earth. In other words, Israel is called to act as God's representative on earth. This will become a key element in the biblical understanding of God's call.

God's command to his people to 'be holy as I am holy' is a command to be like God, to represent who and what he is to the world. He is a loving God, just but merciful, who brings salvation and healing, and the nation's task is to be and to do the same. This vision is a long way from the nationalism that we find in *some* books of the Old Testament, which arises when the command to be holy is interpreted as a command to keep aloof – the interpretation of the relationship between God and his people which we have suggested could be represented by a straight line between two fixed points. What the prophets were insisting was that God's grace did not stop with Israel, but extended to the whole human race. Israel's task was to *reflect* that grace: this is what it meant to act as God's representatives on earth. This task had, according to the story in Genesis 1, originally been entrusted to Adam in the Garden of Eden, and at that time, according to Jewish legend, Adam – created in the image of God – reflected God's glory.[9] No wonder, then, that God's command to his people was to 'be holy as I am holy' – in other words, to be like him. Israel was called to be what Adam had failed to be. The nation's commission was to reveal God to his world – to be a light to the Gentiles, and so bring them to worship him.

What kind of God?

So what *is* God like? What kind of a God was Israel worshipping? According to Richard Dawkins, Israel's God was an extremely nasty piece of work – cruel, unjust, unmerciful, and unreasonable in his demands.[10] It is not a picture that I recognize. To be sure, there *are* passages – as we have already seen – which depict God as a triumphant war-lord, demanding the death of his enemies. They were written by men who understood the demand for holiness to mean the radical rooting out of anything that was *not* 'holy', as they understood that term. But if we turn to the scene in Exodus where God establishes his covenant with Israel, we find a very different picture. God reveals himself to Moses there as

a God merciful and gracious,
slow to anger,

and abounding in steadfast love and faithfulness,
keeping steadfast love for the thousandth generation,
forgiving iniquity and transgression and sin.
                              (Exodus 34.6–7, NRSV)

What God demanded of Israel must reflect this. Not surprisingly, then, we find Micah declaring:

. . . what does the LORD require of you
but to do justice, and to love kindness,
and to walk humbly with your God?
                              (Micah 6.8, NRSV)

But for Christians, the question 'What kind of God?' should be easy to answer, since God has, we believe, revealed himself to us in the person of his Son. Nowhere is this spelt out more clearly than in the Gospel of John. 'The Word became flesh and lived among us, and we have seen his glory' (John 1.14) – seen, that is, what God is like. Here is John expressing the doctrine of incarnation – God becoming man.[11] The true nature of God has been revealed in one who is truly human.[12] It is a doctrine that lies at the heart of our faith, but all too often we do not take it seriously. Artists portray Jesus with a halo, to emphasize his otherness, his holiness, and in the process make him less than human. But the incarnation reminds us that God's holiness is about who he is, and about what he reveals himself to be in the person of Jesus. He is not a God who stands apart, but a God who identifies himself with humanity, a God who gets involved with his creation.

'The Word became flesh and lived among us, and we have seen his glory.' For John, this means that those who have seen Jesus have seen God, and so he depicts Jesus, on the night before his death, telling his disciples, 'Whoever has seen me has seen the Father' (John 14.9). This means, John explains, that the things Jesus says and does are the words and works of God (v. 10). What God says and does are in fact the same thing – as, indeed, the famous opening line of the Gospel reminds us, for when John claims that Jesus is the Logos – the Word – he is referring to a word that is not only spoken but which accomplishes what is said. As Genesis puts it: 'God spoke, and it was so.' It is not so strange, then, that those who believe in Jesus, whom they claim to be 'the truth' (John 14.6), are said, not only to *believe* the truth but to *do* it.[13] Long before, the Psalmist had written:

Teach me your way, O LORD,
That I may walk in your truth.
(Psalm 86.11)

Now the way and the truth are revealed in Jesus, and his followers must 'walk' – that is, live – in accordance with what they see in him.

When I first arrived in Cambridge, many years ago, I inherited a lecture course entitled 'The Theology and Ethics of the New Testament', and found myself lecturing on that theme several times a week. Theology alone, you might have thought, was a big enough topic, needing all the time available, and ethics, too, could easily have filled all the slots allocated to me. But here I was, lecturing on theology *and* ethics, and I soon realized why. Theology and ethics belong together, and refuse to be separated. True, some people assume that religion is all about what they believe, and has nothing to do with everyday life. But theology and ethics, belief and action, belong together, and those who do not *practise* their faith in their daily lives have failed to see the implications of their beliefs. It is no surprise, then, to find Jesus challenging his disciples by asking them, 'Why do you call me "Lord, Lord", and do not do what I say?' (Luke 6.46).

The link between theology and ethics is seen clearly in Jesus' reply to the scribe who asked him which was the greatest commandment. The answer – a quotation from Deuteronomy – appears at first to be straightforward: 'The Lord our God is the one Lord, and you shall love the Lord your God with all your heart, and with all your soul, and with all your mind, and with all your strength.'[14] But Jesus doesn't stop there! He goes on, this time quoting Leviticus: 'The second is this, "You shall love your neighbour as yourself"'[15] (Mark 12.28–34). Surely this is cheating! He was asked for one command, and he has given two. But the reason is clear. The second command is the corollary of the first, and the first cannot be separated from it.[16] If you love God, you *must* love your neighbours, and Jesus maintained that 'neighbours' included Gentiles as well as Jews.[17] As the author of 1 John later insisted, you cannot claim to love God if you hate others.[18] Faith – our trust in God and our love for him – cannot be separated from ethics.

'Justification by faith', the watchword of the Reformation, has dominated Protestant interpretation of Pauline theology for centuries. Sadly, Luther's stress on the antithesis between faith and works as a means of salvation had the unfortunate result that some later interpreters stressed faith to the exclusion of everything else. Personal belief was seen as all-important, and this led to an understanding of religion which concentrated on personal salvation and forgot that – in Paul's words – salvation needed to be 'worked out' (Philippians 2.12) in one's manner of life. Yet Paul is clear that faith is meant to lead to obedience.[19] His mission, he tells the Romans, is 'to bring about the obedience of faith among all the Gentiles' (Romans 1.5).[20] His letters demonstrate how important this obedience – holiness of life – is.

An example of this is seen in what may be Paul's earliest letter, his first epistle to the Thessalonians. According to Acts, Paul's attempt to preach the gospel in Thessalonica had been cut short because of opposition from his fellow Jews.[21] Anxious about the small community of converts he had left behind, Paul sent Timothy to see how they were faring, and when Timothy brought news that their faith was strong, Paul wrote to them expressing his thankfulness.[22] In his opening greeting he reminds the Thessalonians of what their conversion had meant. They had 'turned to God from idols, to serve a living and true God' (1 Thessalonians 1.9). In the last two chapters of the letter, he spells out something of what 'serving a living and true God' meant, and it can be summed up as personal holiness, and concern for one's neighbour. Paul ends the letter with a prayer for the Thessalonian community:

> May the God of peace *sanctify* you entirely, and may your whole spirit and soul and body be kept *blameless* at the coming of our Lord Jesus Christ.
>
> (1 Thessalonians 5.23)

God's demand to his people had been that they should 'Be holy as I am holy'. This command is addressed now to Christians – to those who, as Paul puts it, are 'called to be saints'. They, like Israel before them, are called to be God's representatives on earth – to bring salvation and healing, justice and peace. That is the task to which they have been appointed.

Years ago, when I was a member of a group preparing *The Methodist Service Book* (1975), and was working on the Intercessions, I remember being puzzled by the fact that in every Christian tradition the first prayer is always for the Church. Surely, I thought, we should be praying for everyone else first, and *then* for the Church! Was it not very inward-looking to begin with the Church? A colleague and I produced a draft reversing the usual order, but we were soon shouted down – though I seem to remember that the only reason offered us was 'tradition'! Now, however, I understand the logic. The Church is Christ's body, carrying on his work. We need to pray for the Church, *in order that* we may pray and work for others. The Church must be holy – God's holy people – in order to witness to the world.

Becoming like Christ

For the Christian, the command to 'be holy as I am holy' is a command to be like Christ. Not surprisingly, it is in the letters of Paul that we find the fullest description of what that might mean in terms of everyday life, since Paul was concerned to spell out there what the gospel meant – not simply in matters of belief, but in questions of behaviour. As we have seen, the two belong together, and cannot be separated. For Paul, the reason is that those who respond to the gospel, and who are baptized into Christ, share his death and resurrection. They die to their old way of life, and are raised to a new one – a life that is lived 'in Christ'.[23] That is why they are now truly members of God's people, and that is why Paul addresses them as 'saints', or 'holy ones', the term once used of Israel. The language he uses reminds us of that fundamental relationship between Christ and believers, and of the call to be holy, in a way that our modern use of the term 'Christians' does not.

Another way of expressing this is to say that those who are 'in Christ' are part of a new creation. According to Genesis, Adam had been created after the image of God, but those who belong to Christ have been transferred into a *new* creation,[24] and they are being changed into the image of Christ[25] – who is himself the true image of God.[26] Look at Christ, and you will see what God is like; look at Christians, and what you should see is what Christ is like. For Paul, therefore, the Christian life was a matter of imitating Christ – or rather, of being conformed to Christ.[27] And that is in fact a better way of putting it, since what we are talking about is not merely a matter of imitation – like copying the appearance of the latest celebrity – for it is not something that we can ourselves do, but rather is, for Paul, always the work of the Holy Spirit in the Christian.

If we want to see what this means, there is no better place to look than Paul's letter to the Philippians. This brief letter has something of the nature of a manifesto. Paul is in prison, contemplating a possible death-sentence, and he shares with his friends in Philippi something of his understanding of the gospel, of what it means for their way of life, and of what it has meant for him, as the apostle of Christ. In other words, he sets out here the basis of his mission. Central to the letter is the famous passage in chapter 2 which is sometimes known as the Philippian 'hymn'. Like a hymn – at least the best hymns – it expresses in a structured form something of the significance of the gospel. It tells how Christ,

who was in the form of God,
did not regard equality with God
as something to be exploited,

but emptied himself,
taking the form of a slave,
being born in human likeness.

And being found in human form, he humbled himself
and became obedient to death, even death on a cross.

Therefore God has highly exalted him,
and given him the name that is above every name,

That at the name of Jesus
every knee should bow,
in heaven and on earth and under the earth,

and every tongue should confess
that Jesus Christ is Lord,
to the glory of God the Father.

(Philippians 2.6–11)

Here is a summary of the gospel – of the events that made the
Philippians what they are. One of its many interesting features is
the way that it is introduced and rounded off. Paul is quoting this
passage, not simply to remind the Philippians of the gospel, but to
point out its relevance for their lives. Addressing those who are 'in
Christ', he writes:

> If there is, in Christ, any encouragement, any consolation from
> love, any sharing in the Spirit, any compassion and sympathy . . .
> be of the same mind, having the same love, being in full accord
> and of one mind. Do nothing out of selfish ambition or conceit,
> but in humility regard others as better than yourselves. Let each
> of you look to the interests of others, not to your own. Let the
> same mind be in you that is found in Christ Jesus.

(Philippians 2.1–5)

For many years, New Testament scholars have debated how best
to translate those last few words. The problem is that there is no
verb in the Greek. Literally, it reads 'Think this among yourselves
which also in Christ Jesus.' So is Paul telling the Philippians that
they should have 'the mind that *was* in Christ Jesus' – the mind that
they see reflected in the way in which he behaved?[28] Or is he talking
about the mind which they, the members of his body, already pos-
sess, by virtue of the fact that they are 'in Christ'? As so often, when
confronted with an either/or, the answer may be 'both'![29] The hymn
tells us about what Christ himself did. But Paul's appeal is based
on the assumption that those who are 'in Christ' ought to share
his mind, his attitudes, his love and concern for others. The Revised English Bible's translation attempts to convey this ambiguity:
'Take to heart among yourselves what you find in Christ Jesus.'

At the conclusion of the hymn, he writes, '*therefore*, my beloved,
. . . work out your own salvation' (Philippians 2.12). Working out
their salvation clearly means living out the gospel in their lives –
not just as individuals, but as a community. It means 'being in full

accord and of one mind', and 'doing nothing from selfish ambition or conceit'. But this is not something they do in their own strength, for it is in fact God, Paul reminds them, who is at work in them (v. 13). Nor, indeed, is it simply a matter of their own salvation, since the *result* will be that they will shine like stars in a dark world – a light to others (v. 15).[30]

Paul's mission

Philippians was written by Paul towards the end of his ministry, when he was facing probable death, to Christians who had, he said, shared with him in the gospel from the day they had heard it.[31] Though he may well be referring to the financial support which they have given him,[32] he is surely thinking also of their assistance in *spreading* the gospel. In his letter, Paul not only reminds the Philippians of the gospel and its relevance for their lives, but reminds them, too, of his own ministry, which has been modelled on Christ's self-giving;[33] for this reason he urges them to imitate him.[34] His purpose seems to be to ensure that his understanding of the gospel, and of the Christian community's ministry, is passed on even after his death.[35]

Paul's call to others to imitate him is based on the fact that he is himself the imitator of Christ.[36] For the sake of the gospel, he has endured hunger, thirst, beatings, homelessness, slander, persecution.[37] He is, he tells the Corinthians, 'always carrying in the body the death of Jesus . . . always being given up to death for Jesus' sake'. And so, he concludes, 'death is at work in us, but life in you' (2 Corinthians 4.10–12). Paul's understanding of his apostolic role is that of conformity to the death and resurrection of Christ – and remarkably, he becomes a conveyor of the salvation which comes from Christ: 'death is at work in us, but life in you'. But this is the pattern, not for apostles alone, but for *all* Christian disciples. Paul himself, he tells the Corinthians, has identified himself with Jew and Gentile, with those under the law and those outside the law, has become weak for the sake of the weak, has become all things in turn to all people, for the sake of the gospel.[38] And they are to imitate him!

It is clear, then, that the gospel is spread, not simply by word of mouth, but by *actions*. Writing to the Thessalonians, Paul reminds them how the message of the gospel had come to them, 'not in word only, but also in power' (1 Thessalonians 1.5), because they had seen what kind of people the apostles were – for their sake. It was the *actions* of the apostles, as much as their message, which had impressed the Thessalonians. And they, in turn, became imitators of Paul and of the Lord, and so became an example to others, with the result that the word of the Lord rang out throughout the whole region.

One of the best known of all New Testament stories is that of Paul's conversion on the Damascus Road. In fact, 'conversion' may not be the best term for what happened, since it suggests that Paul was converted from one religion to another, whereas, of course, he continued to worship the same God – the God who, he now believed, had revealed himself in the death and resurrection of Christ.[39] Luke gets so excited by the story that he tells it – at some considerable length – three times over,[40] and in each version of the story he tells us that Paul was called to take the gospel to the Gentiles. Paul himself does not recount the story of the Damascus Road, but in one brief reference to what happened, he recalls the fact that the time came when, as he puts it:

> God, who had set me apart before I was born and called me through his grace, was pleased to reveal his Son in me, so that I might proclaim him among the Gentiles.
>
> (Galatians 1.15–16)

The story, which Luke tells at length, is here contracted to one sentence, and you will have noticed that Paul's account concentrates on the *purpose* of his call – to preach to the Gentiles. But what exactly does he say? 'God . . . was pleased to reveal his Son in me.' Most translators understand Paul to be saying that God was pleased to reveal his Son *to* him, but I suspect that they do so because that is what they think Paul *ought* to have written. Is Paul not describing the revelation of Christ which was given *to* him on the Damascus Road? The problem is that the Greek preposition that Paul uses – the word *en* – normally means 'in'. Was that perhaps what Paul meant? If not, why did he use *en*, rather than the normal Greek construction?

Let us suppose that what Paul intended to say was, indeed, that God was pleased to reveal his Son *in* him, in order that he might proclaim him among the Gentiles. If we are right in doing so, then

Paul understood himself to have been commissioned, not simply to *preach* the gospel, but to *live* it. From that moment the Son of God had, as it were, taken over his life.[41] Indeed, it would seem that Paul believed that it was *necessary* for him to live the gospel in order to preach it: God revealed his Son in him, *in order* that he might proclaim him. Christ was to be revealed *in* him – through his words and actions, his behaviour and his choice of missionary strategy. He can even speak of the fact that 'the marks of Christ' are 'branded' on his body (Galatians 6.17). No wonder, then, that he stresses again and again that what he has done is to try to live in conformity to the gospel.

Paul's so-called 'conversion' was certainly a dramatic turning-point in his life. From now on he was convinced that Jesus was the Messiah and the Son of God, and that God had raised him from the dead. But his 'conversion' can be seen, I suggest, not as a move to a new religion, but rather as a change from one understanding of 'holiness' to another.[42] As a Jew, Paul had been a Pharisee – a term which means 'separated'. Pharisees took the call to be holy seriously, and for Paul, holiness had meant personal piety: living strictly according to the law, avoiding contamination, preserving a relationship with God. This was the 'straight line' model of holiness, linking the holy people with their holy God. But with his call to take the gospel to Gentiles, this understanding of holiness had been destroyed. 'Be holy as I am holy' now meant 'be what I have revealed myself to be in the person of Jesus Christ, who loved you and gave himself up for you'. Now Paul realized that God's holy people were called, not to keep God to themselves, but to take him out into the world, to offer the gospel to the nations, to share their knowledge of a loving and compassionate God. Paul's understanding of holiness has become triangular. It means love of God *and* neighbour – and neighbours are not just his fellow Jews, but the Gentiles.

From the history of both the nation, Israel, and the individual, Paul, we see that God's call to belong to him involves the call to mission. This kind of God cannot be kept to ourselves. Mission is not an optional extra, but is part of a Christian's DNA. Being holy means being like God – the God who, John tells us, loved the world to such an extent that he gave his only Son, so that none should perish (John 3.16). But this mission cannot be limited to the words of preachers or even to personal testimony. The call from God is to *be* holy – and for Christians, that means having the mind of Christ, and becoming like him. It means embodying the gospel, both as individuals and as a community. Mission is not a task to be assigned to a few chosen representatives, but a task for the whole Church, since the Church, as the body of Christ in the world, represents to the world what Christ is. What kind of image of Christ are *we* – as a community – offering to those among whom we live and work?

Notes

1. Preface to *1739 Hymns and Sacred Poems*, in John Wesley, *Works*, Thomas Jackson (ed.), 1829–31, Vol. XIV, p. 321.
2. Similarly Leviticus 19.2; 20.26; cf. Exodus 19.6; 22.31; Deuteronomy 7.6.
3. See in particular IQS – *The Community Rule*.
4. See Philippians 3.4–6.
5. Genesis 12.3; 18.18.
6. Isaiah 43.3, 14; 45.11; 47.4; 48.17; 49.7.
7. Isaiah 2.2–4 = Micah 4.1–3; cf. Isaiah 55.5.
8. Isaiah 55.5; 60.1–3.
9. This is referred to in various Jewish writings, for example in Apoc. Moses (the Greek version of the Life of Adam and Eve) 20–1. By sinning, Adam lost his likeness to God. But in time the hope arose that one day this likeness would be restored, and men and women would once again reflect God's glory. We find this hope expressed in Daniel 12.3 and 2 Corinthians 3.18. According to Exodus 34.29–35, Moses' face shone with the reflected glory of God after speaking to God on Mount Sinai.
10. See, e.g., *The God Delusion*, London: Transworld Publishers, 2006, pp. 268–83
11. Cf. 1 John 1.1–3.
12. Cf. Galatians 4.4; Philippians 2.6–8; Hebrews 1.1–4; 2.5–18.
13. John 3.21. The Greek reads literally 'doing the truth'. Cf. also 1 John 1.6.
14. Deuteronomy 6.5.
15. Leviticus 19.18.
16. To be sure, Paul quotes the 'second' command, saying that it contains 'the whole law', in Galatians 5.14, and makes no reference to the 'first'; cf. also Romans 13.9–10. Love for God is apparently taken for granted. But this is because love for one's neighbours is the corollary which needs to be spelt out.
17. Luke 10.25–37.
18. 1 John 4.20.
19. For the idea that Christians will have to give an account of their actions on the Day of Judgement, see for example 1 Corinthians 3.13–15; 2 Corinthians 5.10.

20. Cf. Romans 15.15–19.
21. Acts 17.1–9.
22. 1 Thessalonians 3.1–13.
23. See Romans 6.
24. 2 Corinthians 5.17.
25. 2 Corinthians 3.18.
26. 2 Corinthians 4.4.
27. Paul uses Greek words meaning 'conformed' in relation to the goal of Christian life in Romans 8.29; Philippians 3.10, 21.
28. This is the way in which the Authorized Version understood it: 'Let this mind be in you, which was also in Christ Jesus.'
29. I have discussed this issue in 'Philippians 2.6–11' in E. Earle Ellis and Erich Grässer (eds), *Jesus und Paulus, Festschrift für Georg Kümmel zum 70. Geburtstag*, Göttingen: Vandenhoeck & Ruprecht, 1978, pp. 151–64; reprinted in *From Adam to Christ: Essays on Paul*, Cambridge: Cambridge University Press, 1990, pp. 88–100.
30. Some commentators believe that Paul is here simply contrasting light with darkness. But echoes of Daniel 12.3, Isaiah 42.6 and 49.6 suggest that he thinks of the Philippians as a source of illumination to others.
31. Philippians 1.5.
22. Philippians 4.15–18.
33. Philippians 3.4–11.
34. Philippians 3.17.
35. I have discussed Paul's purpose in writing the letter in Philippians: 'Phantom Opponents and the Real Source of Conflict' in Ismo Dunderberg, Christopher Tuckett and Kari Syreeni (eds), *Fair Play: Diversity and Conflicts in Early Christianity*, Essays in Honour of Heikki Räisänen, Leiden/Boston: Brill, 2001, pp. 377–95.
36. 1 Corinthians 11.1.
37. 1 Corinthians 4.11–12.
38. 1 Corinthians 9.19–23.
39. The term 'conversion' suggests that Christianity was a separate religion, whereas at the time that Paul became a Christian, it was still a sect within Judaism. Indeed, the terms 'Christian' and 'Christianity' had not yet been coined. Unfortunately the notion that Paul was 'converted' contributed to the later belief that Judaism and Christianity were opposed.
40. Acts 9.1–19; 22.6–21; 26.12–18.
41. Cf. Galatians 2.20.
42. There is an interesting parallel here between Paul and John Wesley, whose 'conversion' is celebrated every year by Methodists – just as Paul's so-called 'conversion' is celebrated by the Church at large. Like Paul, however, Wesley did not 'convert' from one religion to another, nor did he abandon an immoral life for an upright one. Both men had pursued personal holiness *before* their 'conversions'.

2

The Challenge of the City

MORNA HOOKER

According to Professor Robin Dunbar, of the University of Oxford, the human brain cannot cope with more than 150 friendships.[1] Attempt to exceed that number, and social cohesion suffers. Although the manufacturers of my telephone at home have clearly been less than generous in limiting the number of my close contacts to 20 people, the creators of BlackBerry phones and Facebook have, if Professor Dunbar is correct, wildly overestimated the number of people with whom one can have a meaningful relationship.

If the human brain is indeed programmed in this way, it is hardly surprising if our ancestors met problems when they moved out of their Stone Age villages and began to live in cities: there were just too many people for them to cope with. The inevitable results were violent clashes between rival gangs – each of limited size. Those who were not among one's 150 friends were strangers, possibly enemies, even if they lived in the next street. Cities over a certain size were unfriendly places, and the larger the city, the greater the tensions. Big proved to be anything but beautiful. We are familiar with similar problems today. Friends who live in villages tell me how good it is to live in a small community, where it is possible for them to know all their neighbours, and where they are automatically part of a social network. By contrast, those who live in large cities can be desperately lonely.

The truth would seem to be that, though cities are necessary and in many ways convenient, they are not our *natural* environment. According to Genesis, paradise was located in a garden, not a city. To be sure, two human beings could scarcely constitute a city! Nevertheless, the story of Adam and Eve reflects the belief common in the Bible that the garden, rather than the city, is the ideal place in which to live. When the prophets and apocalyptic writers came, at a later stage, to describe what the world would be like when God set it to rights and restored his creation, what they pictured was paradise restored: a return to the Garden of Eden, with nature yielding extraordinarily abundant harvests, men and women – and even animals – living at peace, and everyone sitting contentedly under his or her own fig-tree.

Cities are, by their very nature, unfriendly places, simply because they are too big. Inevitably, they create social divisions. In a city, there must be a division of labour: some will do this, others that – and the 'this' may be considerably more pleasant and enjoyable than the 'that'. In a city, someone must give orders, and others obey. Certain classes – or castes – will perform menial and unpleasant tasks, while others enjoy privileges. The result is a division between ruler and ruled, master and slave, rich and poor, people who matter and those who apparently do not count. No wonder cities create tensions – and in our own day, we see the problems that inevitably result: gang warfare; areas of deprivation and acute poverty; men and women who are living on the streets, or resorting to drugs and alcohol. Surrounded by millions, individuals lose their identity.

Last week, on the way home from a lecture, my train had barely left King's Cross before it came to a full stop – and remained stationary for almost two hours. The reason? The delay was due, we were informed, to 'a fatality on the line'. Some poor soul, overcome by the pressures of life, had decided to end it all. Why, I wondered, had they done so? Was it because of the pressure of living in the modern city? And what had led him or her to commit suicide, not by a private act, but in this particular public way? Was it simply that it seemed to offer a quick fail-safe method? Or was it perhaps a desire to make *some* impact on society? Was it the last, desperate attempt by some lonely soul to make others notice that they had once existed? Certainly their actions affected the lives of several hundred travellers and their friends for a few hours at least, maybe more.

Cities exacerbate problems and create new ones. As if to ensure that we are all aware of the challenge they present, the *Evening Standard* has begun publishing a series of articles on 'Poverty in the City', which it describes as 'A tale of two cities'. Picking up a copy, I found myself reading:

For all the achievement of Londoners and the wonderful things that this city stands for, poverty, homelessness, lack of advantage for dispossessed young people continue to challenge us all.[2]

Judgement

Not surprisingly, cities get a bad press in the Old Testament. The first recorded city is Babel – a name that conjures up in our minds a tower, but the Old Testament story is in fact as much about the city as about the tower, and sadly has nothing at all to say about the tower being toppled. According to Genesis, the descendants of Noah, finding a suitable place in which to settle down, said to one another:

> Come, let us build ourselves a city, and a tower with its top in the heavens, and let us make a name for ourselves; otherwise we shall be scattered over the face of the earth. Then the LORD came down to see the city and the tower, which mortals had built.
>
> (Genesis 11.4–5)

At this time, we are told, the people all spoke the same language, and unity gave them strength, so the Lord regarded their actions as an attempt to become powerful. And because the Lord disapproved, he 'scattered them abroad from there over the face of all the earth, and they left off building the city' (Genesis 11.8). Building a city is not only necessary as a way of finding space for everyone to live; not only convenient – a way of providing food and services for everyone; not only a means of protecting people from their enemies, it is also an attempt to gain power and influence. So one gets rivalry, not only *within* cities, but *between* cities.

Babel is only the first in a long line of cities to be condemned. The names Sodom and Gomorrah were a byword for what was evil and corrupt. And cities in other parts of the world were as bad. Prophets constantly pronounced judgement on them. The book of Nahum, for example, is an oracle against Nineveh. Jeremiah 50–51 pronounces judgement on Babylon. But Jerusalem was no better! Jeremiah announced God's judgement on the city described as ripe for punishment (see Jeremiah 6.6).

From the towns of Judah and the streets of Jerusalem I shall banish all sounds of joy and gladness, the voices of bridegroom and bride, for the whole land will become desert.

(Jeremiah 7.34, REB)

Why? Because the people have refused to worship God, have committed adultery, and have acted unjustly.

Run up and down the streets of Jerusalem,
look around, take note;
search through her wide squares;
can you find anyone who acts justly,
anyone who seeks the truth,
that I may forgive that city?

(Jeremiah 5.1)

The city will be punished because its inhabitants have abandoned both love for God and love for their neighbour. In other words, they have forgotten that they are God's holy people, called to be holy as he is holy.

No wonder the Old Testament prophets denounced the cities! Some of them appear to have seen the cities as the symbol of evil, and hankered after an imaginary, idyllic past – the time when Israel had wandered in the wilderness. Hosea, for example, describes how God is going to speak tenderly to Israel and bring her into the wilderness, saying that she will respond as she did in her youth, at the time when she came out of Egypt.[3] Jeremiah believes that when Israel lived in the wilderness, far from any city, she had been faithful to God.[4] But had she? Other prophets are more realistic about the time in the wilderness – a time when, according to Exodus, Israel had been rebellious. There had certainly been plenty of tensions then – hardly surprising, since Exodus depicts Israel as, in effect, a large mobile city – a large group of people without land, without roots, and with a tendency to break into warring factions.

The prophetic tradition of denouncing cities continues in the New Testament. Jesus pronounces judgement on the small Galilaean cities that he has visited – on Chorazin and Bethsaida, which were, he declared, more wicked than Tyre and Sidon, and on

Capernaum, which was less responsive than Sodom.[5] Although the tower of Siloam had killed a few sinners, there were, he said, many people in Jerusalem who were equally guilty.[6] Jerusalem itself was the city that killed the prophets and which refused to respond to Jesus.[7] The Synoptic Gospels all record his pronouncements of judgement on Jerusalem,[8] and Luke tells us that in his final hours, he urged the grieving women of Jerusalem to weep for themselves, not for him, because of the terrible fate that awaited them.[9]

But the most wicked city of all is 'Babylon' – the pseudonym for Rome – which is described in Revelation 17.5 as the 'mother of whores and of earth's abominations'. And yet – remarkably – the book of Revelation ends with a description of the holy city, the new Jerusalem, which is the home of God himself. The city is built of gold and jewels, and is perfect in its symmetry. From the city flows the river of life, by which grows the tree of life. The Garden of Eden and the city of God have apparently coalesced.

The author of the book of Revelation has clearly picked up another strand in the prophetic tradition – found, for example, in the promises that Sion will be restored,[10] and that the nations will flock to Jerusalem, the city of God, to worship him there.[11] Jerusalem is, after all, as Psalm 48.2 expresses it, 'the city of the great King' – an idea echoed, according to Matthew, by Jesus himself.[12] The temple of God is situated there, so the city is seen as the dwelling-place of God himself. The same tradition appears in the letter to the Hebrews, whose author also speaks of 'the city of the living God, the heavenly Jerusalem' (Hebrews 12.22), 'whose architect and builder is God' (Hebrews 11.10).

The biblical tradition is obviously ambivalent. On the one hand, cities are constantly being denounced: they are places of oppression and injustice. On the other, we have the vision of the holy city, the dwelling-place of God, a vision that inspires both the prophets and the apocalyptic writers, and which depicts men and women living in harmony, not only with God but with one another. What the city is at present – corrupt and evil – is diametrically opposed to what the city will one day be.

Now there are two ways of interpreting these visions of the future. One is to see them as a description of something that lies *beyond* history – a picture of what God himself will establish *after* the Last Judgement. Nothing we can do on earth will have any lasting effect, but at the last day, the present evil order will be swept away, and an entirely *new* order be established. The other is to say: these are visions of what God intended his world – that is *this* world – to be like, and the judgements pronounced by the prophets – and by Jesus himself – are witnesses to the fact that men and women are failing to implement them. If men and women were *truly* obedient – if they loved God and their neighbour, if they were truly 'holy' – then the city would not be a byword for evil, but would embody what God had planned for his world. Our task, then, is not to despair of this world, and dream of a future utopia, but to endeavour to make this world what God intended it to be. True, the task is an impossible one: in spite of all our endeavours, we are not going to build the kingdom of God on earth. But for those of us who live in cities, or who work in cities, as most of us do, the biblical vision of a new Jerusalem is not just a promise, but a summons to action. The task of God's people is to witness to what the city *could* be: a just society, a caring society, where every individual has his or her place, and where all live in harmony. Holiness is about transforming *this* world.

Jesus

But what can we learn from the New Testament about *mission* to the city? According to the Synoptic Gospels, Jesus came to Jerusalem only a few days before his death: the rest of his ministry was spent in Galilee, or in the surrounding regions. In spite of the saying in Matthew which we noted earlier denouncing Chorazin, Bethsaida and Capernaum, the response to Jesus at this time is depicted as overwhelmingly positive. Crowds flocked to him from all the villages and the whole countryside. To be sure, there was opposition. Nazareth could not believe that the man next door could be anything special. Scribes and Pharisees objected to his teaching. Significantly, however, the most vocal of these are said to have come from Jerusalem.[13]

And it is when Jesus reaches Jerusalem that he confronts real opposition. The evangelists all tell us that Jesus was aware of what was likely to happen. Jerusalem had a long tradition of opposing the truth. Luke records Jesus as saying:

I must be on my way, because it is impossible for a prophet to be killed away from Jerusalem. Jerusalem, Jerusalem, the city that kills the prophets, and stones those who are sent to it! How often have I longed to gather your children together, as a hen gathers her brood under her wing, and you were not willing.

(Luke 13.33–34)

Nevertheless, Jesus was determined to go to Jerusalem. Matthew tells us that immediately after Peter's confession of Jesus as Messiah at Caesarea Philippi,

Jesus began to show his disciples that he must go to Jerusalem and endure great suffering at the hands of the elders and chief priests and scribes.

(Matthew 16.21)

Luke tells us that from this point on, Jesus 'set his face towards Jerusalem' (9.51).

For the evangelists, the reason that Jesus went to Jerusalem was simply in order to die. His death and resurrection were the great transforming events in their lives, and they had taken place in Jerusalem. But there was surely more to it than that. Jerusalem was the seat of authority – of *religious* authority – the place where Jewish priests, scribes and Pharisees were to be found. Jesus' message, 'Repent, and believe the good news', had to be addressed to them. But Jerusalem was also a city where Jesus was bound to come into conflict with the Roman authorities. By his presence there, Jesus not only confronted the challenge of the city, but presented a challenge *to* the city. And it was because he challenged the authorities there that he was put to death.

All the Gospels tell us that Jesus entered Jerusalem as a king, riding on the back of a donkey, much as his ancestor Solomon had done.[14] Matthew and John point us to the words of Zechariah 9.9,[15] which suggests that Jesus was entering Jerusalem in peace, an idea picked up by Luke.[16] But Mark, who emphasizes that Jesus *rides* into Jerusalem (an extraordinary thing for a pilgrim coming to a festival to do!) depicts his entry as that of a triumphant king.[17] Here is a challenge to the people to accept Jesus as God's representative – and a challenge, also, to the Roman authorities, to recognize another king beside Caesar. His first action in Jerusalem is to enter the temple and inspect what is happening there. He creates havoc by driving out those who were selling animals for the sacrifices, and by overturning the tables of the money-changers, sending their piles of coins flying. Why? The answer is given in the quotation from Isaiah:

'My house shall be called a house of prayer for all the nations,'
But you have made it a den of robbers.

(Mark 11.17)

The temple needed to be cleansed because the worship that was offered there was hollow. The religious authorities were more concerned to make money from the sale of sacrifices than to worship God: they did not truly love God – and instead of helping others to worship God, they were preventing them from doing so. The temple had been built as a place where not only Israel but *all* the nations could pray, and it was not fulfilling its purpose. No wonder Jesus' action was seen as a sign of the temple's coming destruction! What he was doing was to challenge people to repent and to worship God with heart and soul and mind and strength;[18] but they failed to do so.

In the days that followed, Jesus taught in the temple. Once again, he challenged the religious authorities, this time in a parable about a vineyard, whose tenants refused to give the owner the produce that was his share, and who, when he sent servants and even his son to collect it, killed each of them in turn. The chief priests, scribes and Pharisees, listening to him, realized that he had told this parable against them.[19] They were the tenants who were rebelling against God, refusing to give him the love and obedience they owed him, killing his messengers, the prophets, and plotting to kill his Son.

And now, some Pharisees and Herodians challenge *Jesus*. The extraordinary alliance of Pharisees, whose concern for purity separated them from those Jews who were less strict in their observance of the Law, with Herodians, political supporters of the Roman puppet king, is extraordinary, and demonstrates the danger that Jesus posed. 'Should we pay taxes to Caesar?' they ask. The tax to which they were referring was the poll-tax, and the question was a burning

27

one. The Romans were a foreign power – what right had they to be in Jerusalem? Yet they did maintain law and order. In time, resentment about the tax would result in open rebellion against Rome. But the question posed by Jesus' opponents proves to be a boomerang. 'Show me a coin', he says, 'Whose image is on it?' Jesus' final words, 'Give to Caesar what belongs to Caesar, and to God what belongs to God', is a challenge to his interrogators, and one they are not prepared to meet.[20]

Another challenge came from the Sadducees, who, like the Pharisees, felt threatened by Jesus' teaching; they questioned him about the resurrection. The Sadducees, who were all priests, were an extremely conservative group, who refused to recognize any new revelation of truth. They also insisted that they were right and everyone else was wrong. And Jesus tells them, firmly, that *they* are wrong, and are failing to understand the very scriptures on which they base their beliefs.[21]

These hostile questions remind us of the various groups that were to be found in Jerusalem, and of the tensions that existed there: the only thing that united them was their opposition to Jesus. By contrast, the next incident in Mark's account concerns an honest questioner, who asks him which of the many commandments is the first – the one that sums up all the others. As we have already seen, Jesus is not content to point to one command, but spells out two, since they cannot be separated.

> The first is, 'Hear, O Israel: the Lord our God is the one Lord, and you shall love the Lord your God with all your heart, and with all your soul, and with all your mind, and with all your strength.' The second is this: 'You shall love your neighbour as yourself.'
>
> (Mark 12.29–31)

Jesus has already protested about the failure of the inhabitants of Jerusalem to love God. They have failed to worship him sincerely – and have prevented others from doing so. Like rebellious tenants, they have refused to hand over the rent. They have refused to give God what belongs to God. We are not surprised, then, to find Jesus now warning the people about hypocrites who fail to love their neighbours:

Beware of the scribes, who like to walk about in long robes, and to be greeted with respect in the market-places, and to occupy the best seats in the synagogues and places of honour at feasts. They devour widows' houses and for the sake of appearance say long prayers.

(Mark 12.38–40)

Injustice and sham worship go together.

But not all are guilty. A poor widow comes by and puts into the treasury box at the temple two minute coins. They are all she possesses. She could have offered one and kept the other, but she gives both. Here is a woman who truly loves God with heart and soul and mind and strength, and who loves her neighbour as herself.[22]

Jesus has challenged the religious authorities – and their reaction is to manoeuvre his death. They seize him and present him to the Romans as a traitor against Caesar and a challenge to the Roman power. Jews and Romans alike think that the danger to their authority has been removed. But all is not over. Jesus is crucified as 'King of the Jews'[23] – a challenge not only to the Romans, but to the Jewish nation as well.

Jesus' followers

According to our earliest Gospel, Mark, Jesus begins his ministry by announcing the good news – and then, immediately afterwards, calls four fishermen to be his disciples. 'Follow me,' he demands, 'and I will make you fishers of men' (Mark 1.17). A couple of chapters later, Mark tells us that Jesus appointed twelve disciples.[24] The number twelve is no accident, since it is reminiscent of the twelve tribes of Israel. This small group has been called to be the core of the new Israel: they are representatives of God's holy people. Their task is to be with Jesus, to be sent out to preach, and to exercise authority in driving out demons. This, then, is their mission – to be with Jesus, and so learn what discipleship means; to proclaim the good news; and to bring healing to the sick by driving out demons. The rest of Mark's Gospel has a great deal to tell us about the twelve being 'with Jesus', though they prove slow to learn what discipleship means. A disciple is expected to follow in his master's footsteps: expected to do – and to suffer – what *he* does and suffers.

But the twelve are reluctant to take on board the notion of suffering, and when Jesus talks about taking up the cross, and explains that those who follow him must be prepared to turn their backs on their own interests and to suffer death for his sake, they stop their ears.[25]

In Chapter 6, Mark records how Jesus sent the twelve out, how they preached the gospel, cast out demons, and healed the sick;[26] on their return, they reported their success.[27] A little later in the story, however, we find nine of them failing completely to heal an epileptic child.[28]

As the story reaches its conclusion, Jesus warns four of his followers about the suffering that awaits them as his disciples. Like him, they will be handed over to the Jewish courts, and punished by the religious authorities; they will be summoned to appear before political leaders, also – before governors and kings – and will have the opportunity to witness to them about the gospel. In this way, the gospel will be proclaimed to all the nations.[29]

Mark's Gospel ends, abruptly, at 16.8, with a message to the disciples telling them that Jesus has been raised from the dead, and that he has already gone before them to Galilee. If they wish to see him, therefore, they must follow him there. What happens in Galilee we are not told, but we remember that Galilee was the place where the disciples were called to follow Jesus, and where they were commissioned to go out to preach the gospel, and were given authority over the unclean spirits. Now they are being summoned once again to follow Jesus. In spite of their failure to stand by Jesus in his suffering, and in spite of Peter's denial, Jesus still regards them as his disciples. If they are being summoned to Galilee, will it not be so that he can once again commission them?[30] The good news about Jesus is entrusted to a group of men who had let him down and fled from the Garden,[31] and to a few women who now flee in terror from the tomb!

In his opening verse, Mark told us that he was writing about the beginning of the good news about Jesus Christ. His story about Jesus' ministry has come to an end, but it is only the beginning of a much greater story, and this is the story that the first disciples are going to continue, and which will be carried on by many more Christian disciples after them – even though they may frequently falter and fail.

Certainly that seems to be how Matthew understood what happened, since he tells us that the disciples did indeed meet Jesus in Galilee, and that Jesus sent them out to make disciples of all the nations (Matthew 28.16–20). Luke, in contrast, thinks that the story of Jesus' ministry ended – or perhaps we should say, began again – in *Jerusalem*, but he, too, tells us that Jesus commanded his disciples to take the gospel to all nations (Luke 24.44–49). And Luke, of course, wrote a second volume, the Acts of the Apostles, showing the disciples doing precisely that.

John, too, has what looks like a final encounter between Jesus and his disciples in Jerusalem, where he tells them, 'As the Father sent me, so I send you' – and gives them authority to act in his name by passing on to them the power of the Holy Spirit (John 20.21–22). The statement that they are sent as he has been sent implies that they are to speak and act in the way that he has spoken and acted, an idea that has already been spelt out in the so-called 'Farewell Discourses' in John 13–17, which are introduced by the well-known story of Jesus washing his disciples' feet.

Throughout John's Gospel, we have a series of significant actions – often termed 'signs' – followed by discourses which bring out the meaning of the signs. John 13–17 follows this pattern. Although most of these Johannine signs are miracles, some are dramatic actions that have a significant impact on their audience. So it is here. We are so used to the story of Jesus washing his disciples' feet that we do not appreciate the impact his action would have had. Attempts to re-enact it, in which the feet to be washed have been carefully washed beforehand, or in which 'Maundy money' is distributed, miss the point. Here is Jesus, on his knees, washing feet that were not just dusty but dirty. Unfastening sandals and washing feet were menial tasks which Jewish slaves were not required to do for their masters. Why? A friend who had spent several years in India threw some light on this question when he described how, in rural India, he had regularly seen men and women defecating and urinating by the side of the road. Think back to the days when it was difficult to avoid treading in dog dirt on the pavements, and you will realize the problem. My friend told me that because the feet of passers-by inevitably became contaminated, it was necessary to avoid foot-contact with others. The idea of touching those feet with one's hands was out of the question.

What, I wondered, would have happened in first-century Palestine? If the situation was similar, then one can imagine the shock felt by the disciples when Jesus washed their filthy feet. And one can imagine the horror with which they heard him telling him that they should be doing the same.[32] If this is what the Word made flesh does, if this is what the Holy One does, what should his followers be doing? They are sent, as Jesus himself was sent, to say and do what they saw him say and do.[33]

Surprisingly, the scene in John 20 in which Jesus appears to his disciples after his resurrection is not the last in John's Gospel. John – or someone after him – has added a final chapter, in which Jesus appears to the disciples by the Sea of Galilee. A dramatic account of how the fishermen caught an amazing catch of 153 fish suggests that the time has come for them to begin their role as 'fishers of men', but the conversation that follows is between Jesus and Peter. It is a scene of forgiveness, since Peter, who has denied Jesus three times, is given the opportunity, three times, to affirm that he loves Jesus. But it is also a commissioning, since Peter is instructed to feed Jesus' sheep – and he is warned that this will involve suffering and death. Like his master, Peter is going to glorify God by his death.[34] Jesus' final command is, 'Follow me.'

In the previous chapter, we saw how Paul understood Christian discipleship to mean conformity to Christ. Now we see that all four of our evangelists understood it in the same way. The disciple is required to be with Jesus and to learn from him; the disciple is sent out, as Jesus himself was sent, to preach and live the gospel, and must be prepared to be received in the same manner that he was.

Acts

So how *did* they follow him? Leaving aside the letters of Paul, the main evidence we have is to be found in the account given by Luke in the Acts of the Apostles. Acts can be described as a tale of two cities. It begins in Jerusalem and it ends in Rome, and Luke obviously regards these two cities as having immense significance. Jerusalem was the great city, the city of God, from which the gospel was sent out into the world. Rome was the centre of the Roman Empire, and in spite of being branded as 'Babylon' by the author of Revelation, became the centre from which the gospel would spread into the Western world. Its position as the hub of the Roman Empire, its armies, its trade routes, its efficient system of government, all meant that it provided Christians with unparalleled opportunities to spread the gospel. The book ends with Paul in detention, waiting for judgement – a strange place to end, one supposes, until one realizes that the final words of the book tell us that, in spite of being a prisoner, he was able to proclaim the kingdom of God, and to teach about the Lord Jesus Christ quite openly and without hindrance. In spite of imprisonment and the threat of death, the gospel has reached the heart of the Empire, and nothing will stop it now.

But in between Jerusalem and Rome, Acts mentions many other cities – mostly because they were visited by Paul on his missionary travels. Look at a map, and you will see the immense distances travelled by Paul – and though he walked along the roads built by the Romans, which made travel much easier than it had once been, he could not travel from Philippi to Thessalonica, or from Athens to Corinth, in a day. He would have found it necessary to stop in smaller towns and villages on the way – and I cannot imagine Paul staying the night anywhere without sharing the good news with everyone he met. Acts tells us only about the cities he visited, however – and his letters, also, are written to churches in cities – and with good reason. Like Rome and Jerusalem, these cities were strategic centres. Athens was the intellectual centre of what we now know as Greece – the Oxbridge of its day; Corinth was the commercial centre, through which all trade-routes passed. Travellers were constantly visiting them all: what better way, then, to spread the good news than to establish a Christian community in each city? Form a Christian nucleus in each place, and each one will soon multiply.

Others besides Paul must have adopted a similar policy. The letters to the seven churches in Revelation 1—3 are addressed to Christian communities in seven cities. Until the early twentieth century, establishing small communities in strategic places probably remained the most efficient way to spread the gospel. In a city, it was easy for a preacher to attract a crowd; city missions were packed to the doors. In the twenty-first century, things have changed. The way to spread news now is through radio, television and the web. Whether that is an appropriate – or even a possible – way to share what is essentially a personal relationship with God and with one's fellow men and women is, however, an interesting question. As we have seen, the New Testament suggests that mission is accomplished by *embodying* the gospel, as much as by *proclaiming* it by mouth – and embodying it requires a physical presence. The network of Christian communities is still needed!

The gospel is expressed, not just in word, but in deed. Luke tells us that at the very beginning of his ministry, Jesus announced that in what he was doing, the promises made in Isaiah 61 were being fulfilled: he was bringing good news to the poor, proclaiming release to captives, opening the eyes of the blind, and setting the oppressed free.[35] In Acts, we find the apostles continuing in his footsteps, healing the sick.[36] We find them, too, organizing famine relief,[37] and looking after the poor.[38] Paul constantly urged the members of his churches to help fellow Christians who were in need.[39] I was surprised recently, when responding to the appeal for those who were suffering as a result of the earthquake in Haiti, to find that the envelopes that were distributed in my local church were said to be for contributions to the Methodist World Mission Fund. It was a reminder that mission is not just about *preaching* the gospel, but about *doing* it.

As in the case of Jesus, however, the first disciples of Jesus were not only meeting the challenge *of* the city, but making a challenge *to* the city. Peter and John were brought before the Jewish courts, and were imprisoned for defying them.[40] Stephen denounced the religious leaders, and was stoned to death as a result.[41] They came up against the political authorities, too. Herod executed James,[42] and imprisoned Peter.[43] Paul was brought before Jewish courts and before the Roman authorities.[44] If the political powers opposed the work of God, then they themselves had to be opposed.

It has often been suggested that Luke, in writing Acts, was endeavouring to show that Christianity was not really subversive, and that Rome need not worry about the Church's message. If so, he was apparently agreeing with Paul, who in Romans 13 urged the Romans to respect the authorities and to obey those who governed them. Both Luke and Paul regarded the Roman Empire as a force for good, since it gave stability to a world which would otherwise have fallen into chaos. A petty tyrant like Herod was another matter altogether. And in time Rome itself abused its powers, persecuting the Church, which explains why the author of Revelation regarded it as the devil incarnate. When religious authorities and

34

political powers opposed the truth of the gospel, then both had to be resisted. Today, it may well be that for us, too, 'mission' means not just meeting the challenge *of* the city, but presenting a challenge *to* the city, wherever we see corruption and injustice. If those whose duty is to uphold justice fail to do so, they must be withstood.

The good news announced in the opening chapter of Matthew's Gospel is 'Emmanuel',[45] God with us. This is God's method of communicating – not sending a message, but coming in person. God speaks to us by coming among us; for, as the Fourth Evangelist puts it, Jesus is the Word made flesh.[46] In thinking about mission – that is about being sent – we remember that we, Jesus' disciples, are sent, as he himself was sent, to *be* God's presence in the world – sent to *embody* the gospel.

Notes

1. Robin Dunbar, *How Many Friends Does One Person Need?*, London: Faber & Faber, 2010.
2. A comment by Prince William on the *Evening Standard*'s 'Report on Poverty', quoted in the *Evening Standard* for 2 March 2010.
3. Hosea 2.15.
4. Jeremiah 2.2.
5. Matthew 11.21–23.
6. Luke 13.4.
7. Matthew 23.37–38.
8. Matthew 24; Mark 13; Luke 21.5–36.
9. Luke 23.27–31.
10. Isaiah 60.1–7; 62.10–12.
11. Isaiah 2.2–4 = Micah 4.1–3; Isaiah 60.7.
12. Matthew 5.35.
13. Mark 3.22.
14. 1 Kings 1.32–48.
15. Matthew 21.4–5; John 12.15.
16. Luke 19.38.
17. Mark 11.1–10.
18. Mark 12.30.
19. Mark 11.27; 12.12.
20. Mark 12.13–17; Matthew 22.15–22; Luke 20.20–26.
21. Mark 12.18–27; Matthew 22.23–33; Luke 20.27–38.
22. Mark 12.41–44.
23. Mark 15.26. Mark emphasizes Jesus' kingship throughout his account of the crucifixion: 15.2, 9, 12, 16–20, 26, 32.

24. Mark 3.13–19.
25. Mark 8.31–38.
26. Mark 6.6–13.
27. Mark 6.30.
28. Mark 9.14–29.
29. Mark 13.9–13.
30. For the implications of Mark's ending, see Morna D. Hooker, *Endings: Invitations to Discipleship*, London: SCM Press, 2003; Peabody, MA: Hendrickson, 2003, pp. 11–30.
31. Mark 14.50.
32. John 13.14–15.
33. John 20.21. God's purpose in sending his Son was, we are told, to save the world (3.17).
34. John 21.18–19.
35. Luke 4.16–21.
36. Acts 3.1–10; 8.7; 14.8–18.
37. Acts 11.27–30.
38. Acts 2.45; 6.1–6.
39. See, for example, 2 Corinthians 8.
40. Acts 4.1–7; 5.17–41.
41. Acts 7.
42. Acts 12.1–2.
43. Acts 12.3–11.
44. 2 Corinthians 11.24; Acts 16.19–40; 21.27–26.32.
45. Matthew 1.23.
46. John 1.14.

3

Being Holy in the Cities of the Roman Empire

FRANCES YOUNG

The premise of this chapter is that we can learn from history – not by literally copying what has been done in the past, because circumstances are always different, but by allowing those differences and similarities to challenge us into a new perspective on our own situation. The idea is that an exploration of the position of Christians in the pre-Christendom world might provide interesting analogies and possibilities for Christians in a post-Christian society as we consider what the Church's mission might be. I will concentrate on the history but in such a way as to open up such possibilities for consideration.

Christianity spread through cities: Antioch, where Christians were first named as such; the Greek cities on the seaboard of Asia Minor – Ephesus, Pergamum, Smyrna, together with the others of Revelation's seven cities; the cities that Paul went to, inland in Asia Minor, on the seaboard of the Aegean, Corinth, Rome; other great cities of the Roman Empire like Alexandria, Carthage and Lyons. The city in this Graeco-Roman world was identified with civilization; the Greek word for 'city' is *polis*, from which we get 'politics', and the city was the key focus of loyalty and participation, benefactions, rivalries, competition for favours. Despite Roman dominance the cities had a measure of independence, with considerable local autonomy and influence over their hinterland. The highly positive view of the city usual in this culture may be contrasted with the negative aspects of the picture found in the previous chapter. It was through the cities and their trading networks that Christianity, like other movements, spread. In the period before the first Christian Emperor, Constantine, there is almost no evidence of Christianity in the rural backwaters of the Empire, and after Constantine it was very slow to displace traditional religion in the countryside. That non-Christians came to be called 'pagans' is an indicator – *pagani* is the Latin for 'countryfolk'. The importance of the city context will become clear as we proceed.

The character of the Christian community

To begin our exploration of what it meant to be Christian in the cities of the Roman Empire, let me quote a sketch of an exemplary Christian community written at the turn of the first century:

> Anyone who paid you a visit affirmed the quality and steadiness of your faith, admired your balanced Christian devotion and broadcast the generous character of your hospitality . . . With humility and total lack of arrogance, at the service of others rather than demanding attention, and gladly giving rather than receiving, you were all satisfied with what Christ had provided, attended carefully to his words, treasuring them in your hearts, and keeping his sufferings before your eyes. In this way a deep and rich peace was granted to everyone, along with an insatiable desire for doing good, and a full outpouring of Holy Spirit came upon all. Holiness was your intent as you stretched out your hands to Almighty God, with enthusiasm for goodness and devout confidence, praying that God would be merciful if you had inadvertently sinned.[1]

Such was the character of this Christian group: its emphases indicate continuity with the picture we find in the New Testament. Holiness is the prime Christian calling, which is taken to mean avoiding sin – indeed, the notion that post-baptismal sin was unforgivable would become a major issue quite quickly and eventually lead to the development of a penitential system. If one looks carefully it also becomes clear that keeping a low profile is turned into a virtue. There are good reasons for thinking that being holy in the cities of the Roman Empire meant Christians separating themselves from the world, rather than engaging in public proselytizing. So how did Christianity spread? And what did Christians think their mission was? Before we turn to those questions, we need a brief sketch of how Christians and their groups might be perceived in that social context.

In the cities of the Roman Empire Christians were

- known as *Christianoi*, the Latinate form suggesting followers of a political faction;
- called 'atheists' – they separated themselves from all contact with traditional religion: civic festivals, the imperial cult, and much ordinary social life, by their conscientious objection to offering sacrifice and incense to the gods;
- called the 'third race' – that is, neither Jews nor Greeks,[2] 'Greeks' standing for all the Gentile populations of the Roman Empire.

They belonged to something

- a bit like a club or *collegium*, meeting for meals, with their own private rituals, making provision for the burial of members and the remembrance of their dead – rumours circulated about what they got up to: incest and cannibalism were prime candidates;
- a bit like a mystery cult, promising immortality through initiation into secret night-time rituals; as members of such a cult they were seen as devotees of some new-fangled superstition, inviting a government ban if they caused public disturbances as Dionysiacs had;
- a bit like a household – a group would meet in a house and behave like an extended family, patriarchally ordered yet familiar with each other (calling each other father, brother, sister), with an *episcopos* (or head steward) to manage things, directing the *diakonoi* (or servants) who served at table, and with arrangements to support orphans, widows and elders (*presbyteroi*) whose age and experience gave them respect and influence as they conserved the community's memory;
- a bit like small groups of Diaspora Jews (in this period Jews were dispersed around the cities of the Mediterranean and the Middle East), gathering in houses adapted as synagogues, reading and learning from scriptures, offering 'spiritual sacrifices' through prayer and almsgiving rather than having temples, with strict purity regulations and ethical norms;

- very like a school of philosophy, with teachers who advocated a particular lifestyle, backed up by an account of the truth about how things are (that is teachings, doctrines) as a warrant to justify the behaviour advocated, and with public readings of ancient books, in which those teachings were found if properly interpreted; yet this was unlike other schools, which were usually elitist, in that all comers were welcome – the poor, slaves, women, outcasts, orphans, widows.

In other words, Christians were an anomaly in the social world of the Roman Empire's cities. One imperial edict reflects the difficulty of categorizing them by calling them a nation (*ethnos*), then a superstition (*deisidaimonia*) and then a cult (*thrēskeia*).[3] They simply didn't fit obvious categories, though combined several to some degree. Indeed, Christianity was not obviously a religion at all – its eventual success not only displaced other religious practices but also modified for ever the understanding of what religion is.

Religion in the Roman Empire

Perhaps that anomalous character can provide clues to the Church's mission in those early centuries. We will consider how Christianity spread in the Roman Empire, why it spread and what its message was. But first we need to clarify various things about that context – especially its religious character:

- Religion in the Roman Empire was everywhere and, in a sense, nowhere. In other words, it was never a separate category from everyday life. At home there were the household/ancestral gods, acknowledged by habitual rituals. Clubs and trades had special deities who would look after their interests if properly honoured with gifts. Each city had its own patron gods, served by municipal priests, often elected officials, with their temples dominating public space and their festivals providing great public holidays. The military had their standards surrounded with religious honours; and there was the Ruler-cult – cities in Asia Minor, for example, competed with each other in building temples and offering honours to the Emperor.[4] There were famous healing shrines where people would go and sleep in sacred spaces hoping for miracle cures or prescriptions in dreams as an answer to prayer. Then there were all kinds of exotic foreign gods and mystery cults, with promises of benefits for their worshippers, notably immortality. People who went over the top in getting out divine insurances of all kinds were lampooned as superstitious, but intellectuals, while offering critiques of the gods and their myths, recognized the importance of religion to society and went along with it. It was a matter of practice not belief, of binding duties (the root meaning of the word *religio* lies here) which bound families to their ancestral gods and the state to the unseen powers that had made Rome great.

- Religion tended to follow ethnicity. The cities of the Roman Empire have been described as each a great melting-pot. It is true that few had a static population, that there was constant coming and going and most people lived in cramped tenement houses – indeed the density of population was probably higher than any modern city. (Of course, it is hard to estimate, but with a total population of about 1 million, give or take 200,000, Rome's density has been calculated as between 200 and 300 per acre, thus topping the density of Bombay and Calcutta (in the 1990s 183 per acre and 122 respectively).)[5] Antioch seems to have had 18 different ethnic quarters in Roman times;[6] to a large extent religion followed ethnicity and so local cults spread with migration. However, melting-pot is not quite the right description: there is ample evidence that mostly people stuck within their ethnic groups, imported their home-cults and there was very little mixing or melting.

- There was no such thing as a missionary religion before Christianity. Lots of cults did expand, both through urban societies around the Mediterranean and through the Roman legions as they moved from one end of the Empire to the other, attracting adherents who simply added another one to other religious practices, or dropped it as they fancied. There was no exclusive commitment, no conversion as such. It was once assumed that Jews sought proselytes in the sense of seeking to get Gentiles to convert to Judaism, but that idea is now discredited.[7] It is clear that synagogues did attract

non-Jews, and occasionally people who took on the whole
Jewish way of life; but effectively they were becoming part
of a different ethnic community, with different ancestral cus-
toms, and probably the most common reason for this was
marriage into the community.

• Rome respected the ancestral religions of the peoples over
which it ruled, including that of the Jews. Ethnicity and
antiquity guaranteed the respectability of a religion. Christianity stood outside those criteria, and furthermore lured people
away from their proper religious obligations whether Jewish
or otherwise. As the 'third race' they belonged neither to the
polytheistic majority nor to the exception that proved the rule –
the Jewish community which would not compromise or conform on ancient and traditional grounds.

The spread of Christianity

Keeping that background in mind, which again implies the anomalous position of Christian groups in Roman society, what can we
say about the spread of Christianity? It was clearly felt to be phenomenal, indeed providential. Towards the end of the second century Bishop Irenaeus could speak of the Church as being dispersed
throughout the whole world, even to the ends of the earth;[8] in the
middle of the third century, Origen could refer to the multitude of
people coming to the faith, even rich people and persons in posi-
tions of honour, ladies of refinement and high birth;[9] by the early
fourth century, Eusebius could look back to the beginnings and
write:

> Thus with the powerful co-operation of Heaven the whole world
> was suddenly lit by the sunshine of the saving Word . . . In every
> town and village, like a well-filled threshing floor, churches shot
> up bursting with eager members. Men who through the error they
> had inherited from generations of ancestors were in the grip of
> the old spiritual sickness of idol-worship, by the power of Christ
> and through the teaching of his followers and the miracles they
> wrought were freed, as it were, from cruel masters and found
> release from galling fetters. They turned their backs on devil-
> ish polytheism in all its forms and acknowledged there was one

God only, the Maker of all things. Him they honoured with the ordinances of true religion through that divine reasonable worship of which our Saviour sowed the seed in the life of men.[10]

Modern historians have also thought the rate of expansion so extraordinary as to need explanation.[11] So how did Christianity spread, and why?

Public preaching

The obvious answer would be public preaching missions like those of Saint Paul. Indeed, when an opponent asserted, 'If all wanted to be Christians, the Christians would no longer want them', Origen replied, 'Christians leave no stone unturned to spread the faith in all parts of the world', and describes people 'going around not just cities but villages to make others pious towards God'.[12]

However, there are difficulties with generalizing this. The first concerns the nature of Paul's activity, which according to Acts was rarely conducted as an open-air soap-box proclamation – the speech on the Areopagus is the exception that proves the rule: generally Paul went to the local synagogue first and did not, like John Wesley in the eighteenth century, 'consent to become more vile' and engage in field preaching. The second problem is the general lack of evidence for other such open preaching missions.[13] It was, after all, positively dangerous: 'If anyone does still wander about in secret [missions], . . . he is sought out and condemned to death', wrote that same opponent, Celsus, in the late 2nd century; and a bit later Christians could be described as 'a tribe obscure, shunning the light, dumb in public though talkative in corners'.[14] For good reason Christians mostly kept a low profile, though there are stories suggesting that they turned out in crowds to support martyrs, the point being that the authorities thought the thing to do to suppress a movement was to attack leaders, not the rank and file.

There is a good deal of evidence of travelling teachers, against whom congregations are warned in much early Christian literature[15] – indeed, their propensity to sponge off Christian groups is beautifully caricatured by one second-century satirist;[16] but clearly these itinerants mostly visited churches and taught those already converted, rather than conducting public evangelistic campaigns. There are occasional references to prophets in market-places behaving like Cynic philosophers;[17] and there is a narrative of a fresh evangelistic mission around AD 250: Gregory, known as Thaumaturgus (the Miracle-Worker), travelled to the highlands and backwaters of what we now call Turkey (Cappadocia and Pontus), preached to crowds and brought large numbers into the Church, but it has been noted that mostly teaching was given after converts were won by astounding miracles and exorcisms.[18]

The power of miracles

Indeed, the claim has been made that what a religion needed to spread in the Roman world was blatant evidence of power, so actually miracles and magic rather than preaching lay at the basis of the phenomenal spread of Christianity: this alone can explain mass conversions.[19] To quote Harnack's classic, 'exorcism formed one very powerful method of their mission and propaganda'.[20] In the third century, in fact, Origen suggested that 'without miracles and wonders [the apostles] would not have persuaded those who heard new doctrines and new teachings to leave their traditional religion and accept [these] teachings at the risk of their lives', and admits that Christians 'still charm daemons away and perform many cures'.[21]

Numerous stories coming from various dates are told of

- direct confrontation with daemons (that is, pagan gods) in which the Christian exorcist clearly prevails – with temples or oracles crippled. On one occasion, for example, the sign of the cross was secretly put on the foreheads of animals to be sacrificed, and as a result the soothsayers could not read the auspices for the Emperor;[22]
- possessed individuals healed by exorcism. In Egypt, for example, Saint Antony is said to have challenged certain wise pagans to heal some people suffering from possession, by using rational argument or any other skill or magic they liked and calling on their idols, or else to acknowledge the power of Christ's cross. He then called on Christ, sealed the sufferers

with the sign of the cross three times, and they were healed;[23]
- effective prayer ending drought, for example, and so crowds flocking to the churches;
- the martyrs' defiance of death making people wonder what was at the back of it; or other associated marvels. In 305 a victim of persecution was killed by drowning. There followed an earth tremor and the sea washed up the body. The whole population of the town attested this miracle, we are told, believed God's wrath was upon them and confessed the one and only God of the Christians.[24]

Opponents of Christianity, like Celsus in the second century, openly accused Christians of being magicians.[25] It was a charge Christians resisted,[26] maintaining that they used only prayer, the power of Jesus' name or the sign of the cross, not magical arts or sorcerers' devices; yet the discoveries of magical papyri in Egypt show how easily Christian terminology was added to other supposedly powerful names to deliver the spell's desired effects. Like magic, prayers and offerings were supposed to be powerful enough to deliver what people desired, and mainly what they prayed for was health, good crops, safety when embarking on risky journeys, or foreknowledge of the future.[27] A god powerful enough to produce effects in the world was to be respected, and rumours of the Christians' nocturnal sacraments, esoteric signs and the magic name of Jesus would attract the desperate. In other words, the argument runs, it was not their teaching or preaching, but their apparent access to supernatural power that gave Christians the edge.

Networks

However, it may be that the supposed 'inconceivable rapidity'[28] of Christianity's spread could turn out to be not so extraordinary after all. A sociologist, Rodney Stark, used standard calculations of the number of Christians and the proportion of the total population who were Christian at a sequence of dates, and concluded that the expansion was about 40 per cent per decade, which compares very closely with the spread of Mormonism.[29] Research has shown that Mormons have expanded, not through their endeavours to convert on doorsteps or engage in other public activities, but through open networks and personal contacts.

This observation dovetails with key evidence about Christianity in the early centuries. A second-century letter to an enquirer stated:

> The difference between Christians and the rest of humankind is not a matter of nationality, or language or customs. Christians do not live apart in separate cities of their own, speak a special dialect, nor practise any eccentric way of life . . . They pass their lives in whatever township – Greek or foreign – each person's lot has determined; and conform to ordinary local usage in their clothing, diet, and other habits . . . To put it briefly, the relation of Christians to the world is that of a soul to the body. As the soul is diffused through every part of the body so are Christians through all the cities of the world . . . The soul, invisible herself, is immured within a visible body; so Christians can be recognized in the world, but their Christianity itself remains hidden from the eye.[30]

Here the Church as an organization is acknowledged to be 'underground' and subject to opposition, but Christians permeate society. Our second-century opponent spoke of them being a secret society, made up of 'wool-workers, cobblers, laundry-workers' and such like, who 'in private houses' get hold of women and children and encourage them to ignore 'their father and their schoolmasters' and 'go along . . . to the wool-dresser's shop, or to the cobbler's or the washerwoman's shop, that they may learn perfection'.[31]

Exploring this network theory, Stark argues (i) that the Jewish Diaspora networks evidently used by Paul remained important in the cities of the Roman Empire, the proximity of synagogues and houses converted to churches being good evidence; (ii) that Christians did not come from the lowest of the low in Roman society, any more than they came from the tiny elite at the top – rather they came from artisans and traders, immigrants and people whose place in society was a bit ambivalent, just the sort who would be drawn into a tight organization which provided status, security and belonging; (iii) that women provide an important key to Christianity's spread[32] – evidence shows that a number of high status women were attracted, the rule against divorce had priority over the encouragement not to marry out, and indeed imbalance of numbers as well as social status meant women often did marry out and sometimes produced 'secondary conversion' of their husbands; and furthermore, because Christians opposed abortion and exposure of infants, their population increased at a faster rate than others. Word of mouth and reputation drew people in; kinship and connections made this possible.

In other words, while exploiting existing networks, Christians also created new ones. It is no accident that the predominant genre of early Christian literature is the letter – some may have been imitations of Paul's letters, but most are real correspondence addressed to churches in the major cities of the Empire. A considerable catalogue of named early Christians who travelled can be assembled,[33] and given that a large proportion of the membership may well have been traders (examples include Aquila and Priscilla in the first century, Marcion in the second), the networks enabled itinerants to find a spiritual home wherever they touched down. Many would lodge in cramped tenements, but churches were usually based in households – it has been calculated that the average household consisted of 50 persons, given the extended family, the servants and slaves, clients and tenants (a typical urban house, with its inner courtyards, had shop-fronts onto the street). Needless to say, the 'patriarch' of such a household, who allowed the meetings to take place there, would be in a strong leadership position; but would also no doubt be part of a network of such households in a big city like Rome.[34] Invitations offered to contacts would be the principal way in which household groups expanded and Christianity spread.

The way in which Christianity spread, then, seems to have been through open and overlapping networks.

So why were people attracted?

Belonging and practical support

First and foremost, no doubt, was membership of a community where people found status and a sense of belonging. But for some there was concrete, practical, even financial support in a society where there were no safety nets. By the middle of the third century we find evidence that in Rome Christians supported 46 presbyters, 7 deacons, 7 sub-deacons, 42 acolytes, 52 exorcists, readers and doorkeepers, and more than 1,500 widows and distressed persons.[35] Doubtless word got around among people struggling to make a life in cramped and inhospitable cities. Positive earthly benefits had the power to attract. Tertullian speaks of a common fund used to feed and bury poor people, support orphans and the old, help those shipwrecked or sentenced to the mines, prison or exile.[36] There is even a suggestion that the Church itself provided work for those (such as actors or soldiers) who gave up their profession because of their Christian commitment.[37] Churches in various locations also supported each other, sometimes with practical help (Paul's collection for the Jerusalem church was but the first of a number we know about) but also with intercession.[38]

Reputation for care for the sick

We should not underestimate the level of ill-health and the low life expectancy of the ancient world. Despite aqueducts, baths and public latrines, there was an almost total lack of clean water, sanitation and rubbish disposal in the crowded tenements, where the masses lived; filth, stench, flies, mosquitoes and disease were endemic in pre-modern cities. So one of the things people wanted from religion was health – there was no 'secular' medicine: Galen, the medical philosopher whose writings have come down to us, learned his medicine at a massive pilgrimage site in Pergamum, where people flocked for healing from the god Asklepios.[39] But only the elite got to the spas! One way and another Christians got a reputation for being able to assist – we have already commented on the power of a reputation for miracles and healing.

The Empire suffered more than one massive epidemic in this period, with loss of population and considerable social breakdown. Between the years 165 and 180, for example, somewhere between a quarter and third of the population, including the Emperor Marcus Aurelius, were lost to what may have been the first appearance of smallpox in the West, and in 251 there began another devastating epidemic.[40] At the time Christians suggested that these terrible events actually helped their cause. Around the year 260, Dionysius, Bishop of Alexandria, wrote:

Most of our brother Christians showed unbounded love and loyalty, never sparing themselves and thinking only of one another.
Heedless of danger they took charge of the sick, attending to
their every need and ministering to them in Christ, and with them
departed this life serenely happy; for . . . many in nursing and
curing others, transferred their death to themselves and died in
their stead . . . death in this form, the result of great piety and
strong faith, seems in every way the equal of martyrdom.[41]

Dionysius reckoned that in every house there was at least one dead,
but the full impact fell on the heathen, who

> behaved in the opposite way. At the first onset of the disease, they
> pushed the sufferers away and fled from their dearest, throwing
> them into the roads before they were dead and treating unburied
> corpses as dirt, hoping thereby to avert the spread and contagion
> of the fatal disease.

Tertullian had noted some 60 years earlier that opponents observed,
'Look how they love one another',[42] and in the midst of dire
plague Dionysius reports them doing just that. And so the community enabled people to survive and recover, their mortality rate
was lower, and in the aftermath people would have acknowledged
the power of the Christian God. Rumours of miraculous survival
would attract, and some degree of stability in the midst of social
panic would have an effect.

Cyprian, Bishop of Carthage around 250,[43] commented on how
the plague sorted out who was really just and good: whether the
well cared for the sick, whether relatives loved their kin as they
should, whether masters showed compassion for ailing slaves,
whether physicians deserted their patients. In other words, Christians could provide a purpose or explanation for the event where
pagans were just perplexed. But they could also provide consola-
tion for the bereaved.

Contempt for death

Perhaps the most challenging thing about Christians was their
contempt for death, evidenced in their behaviour when faced by

epidemics, but also in their willingness to go to martyrdom. This contempt for death was grounded in their confident hope of immortality or resurrection. Our second-century satirist comments:

> The poor souls have convinced themselves that all will be immortal and will live for ever, on account of which they think lightly of death and most will surrender to it voluntarily.

Galen too said,'their contempt of death is patent to us every day'.[44]

In the aftermath of the massive, Empire-wide persecution in 250, Cyprian was besieged by lapsed Christians desperately demanding readmission to communion. They had allowed themselves to offer incense to the Roman gods as required by the authorities, or had somehow obtained certificates to say they had and so avoided confessing Christ, with its attendant risk of martyrdom. What lies behind this situation? The old textbooks used to speak of 'nominal' Christians, but what would 'nominal' mean before Christianity constituted normality? The likelihood is that a good many people had done the usual thing of taking out a variety of religious insurances, thought Christ was a god worth cultivating for the sake of life after death and after years of toleration simply had not reckoned with the exclusive loyalty demanded of a Christian. Once the crisis was over they started to worry about their eternal destiny – for they were being deprived of the 'medicine of immortality', as Ignatius had called the Eucharistic elements. This episode is particularly instructive when it comes to understanding why people were attracted to Christianity. Clearly people were attracted by the offer of health for body and soul and the promise of immortality. Bishops and pastors, like Christ himself, are frequently described as physicians able to apply the right medicines for the ailments of the soul.[45]

All this tends to endorse MacMullen's view that it was not because of active public missions, nor because of the content of its message, that Christianity spread – neither made the first impact. However, if we ask what Christians thought they were about, content immediately becomes important, and the bishop's medicine was often identified as the teaching of the truth. Once someone arrived at the house or shop where Christians were meeting, they would be taught things, and it would be the combination of that teaching with the sense of belonging and support which would hold them.

So what were Christians trying to communicate?

The monarchy of God

The most obvious and most fundamental teaching was the 'monarchy' of the one God who created all things, and the need to turn 'from idols to serve the living and true God' (which is how Paul described the outcome of conversion in 1 Thessalonians 1.9). One might be tempted to think that was just a continuation of Jewish mission, but it has been shown convincingly that Jews did not set out to proselytize in this period, and did not expect Gentiles to abandon polytheism.[46]

There were Gentile sympathizers attracted to Judaism, and the book of Acts suggests that it was these Gentiles who responded to Paul's teaching in the synagogues. The Jews were respected, by philosophers and as philosophers, [47] for their wisdom, which included monotheism – philosophers had long been developing the notion of one ultimate divine being, though it tended to be a rather abstract concept, and also for their practise of virtue. They were admired for the 'intellectual' gatherings in their synagogues – evidenced not only in their ethical and religious debates but their 'spiritual worship', prayer without sacrifices or images. But Jews did not set out to attack the religion of others – rabbis even made provision for Jewish craftsmen to manufacture what Gentiles needed for their worship.[48] Christians, however, definitely did attack idolatry: the vehemence of their opposition to paganism has been described as 'noticeable and reprehensible'.[49]

The folly of idolatry is the first thing Christians turned to in their explanatory and apologetic literature, exploiting both the critique long since offered by Greek philosophers, and also the scriptures, such as Isaiah's famous satire proving the idols are nothing: the craftsman uses part of the felled tree to make a fire, warm himself and cook, another part to carve a god (Isaiah 44.9–20). They mocked the idols as powerless: 'Christians say, Look, I stand by the image of Zeus or Apollo, or any god indeed, and I blaspheme it and strike it; but it takes no vengeance on me', states our second-century critic.[50] Christian attacks on idolatry and the refusal of these mostly non-Jews to have any truck with traditional religion lay at the heart of their vulnerability in Graeco-Roman society – Jews were exempt because their ancestral religion, with its peculiar exclusivity, was recognized. The biggest life-changing aspect of conversion was withdrawal from pagan worship.

The teaching about the one God was a point that placed Christians, like Jews, in the category of philosophers. In both cases, meetings were more like school gatherings than religious assemblies. Books were read and interpreted. Ethics and the truth about life, the universe and everything was expounded and discussed. The story of the Roman Church in the second and third centuries is plausibly written in terms of teachers setting up philosophical schools in their homes.[51] Justin Martyr is a good example, but not the only one – in the account of his martyrdom we are told that he stated, when pressed, that Christians had no single meeting-place, but some met in his home 'above the baths', where he also lived and taught.[52]

Now the Greek word 'monarchy' has a double sense: *archē* may mean 'beginning' or 'first principle', or it can mean 'rule'. The insistence on God's monarchy in Christian theology implied both. So the sole 'monarchy' or rule of God had universal and potentially political implications. On the one hand, Christians had a self-understanding of being 'citizens of heaven' and so dispersed as aliens in the kingdoms of this world;[53] on the other hand, everything was subject to God's providence, and Christians could argue that the emperor was only emperor because God had put him there – indeed they quickly noted the point that the united Empire under Augustus had arisen at the same time as Christianity, and would sooner or later suggest that that was providential in that it facilitated the spread of Christianity.[54] Christians, like Jews, could plead that they were good citizens in the very fact that they prayed for the emperor and civil authorities; and they certainly did not engage in wrongdoing, recognizing, as they did, that Roman laws were established under God to protect people and ensure justice. Indeed, the second-century apologists showed considerable devotion to the monarchy,[55] and tended to treat the emperors as philosopher-kings who, if only they knew what Christianity was really about, would soon recognize Christians were undeservedly punished; Origen thought the emperors ruled by divine right and monarchy was the best form of government.

But this sense of the universal providence of the one true God also fuelled opposition to the pluralist religious assumptions of the majority, set up potential conflict with the Ruler-cult and generated urgency in getting people to recognize that truth, since in the long run everyone would be judged accountable to this God. Indeed, one of the most striking things in the earliest literature outside the New Testament, the Apostolic Fathers, is that sense of accountability to a God who even sees the secrets of the heart:

> Let us observe how close God is, and that none of our thoughts, none of the inner debates we have, escape his attention. Awe and respect for the Lord is a beautiful thing, a real bonus, bringing salvation to all who live with that attitude, with a pure mind and holy lifestyle. For God is a searcher of thoughts and desires. We have his breath in us, and when he wills, he will withdraw it.[56]

> Nothing escapes the Lord's notice – indeed, even our hidden secrets are present to him. So let us act in everything we do as if he were dwelling within us, so that we may be his temples and he may be our God within us.[57]

With this universalistic belief in accountability to the one and only God and the expectation of judgement, there would be strong motivation for getting friends and loved ones to come along to Christian assemblies to learn what the truth is.

The fulfilment of prophecy

The second most important element in the message of the early Christians concerned the fulfilment of prophecy. Several comments are worth making.

First, this was an astute move in terms of the culture. Ancient religious myths were full of riddling oracles, the interpretation of their double meanings, or their misinterpretation and the dénouement (one only has to think of the Oedipus story). Everyone wanted to know what the future held for them, particularly when undertaking a risky operation; to meet the demand there were soothsayers, famous shrines had oracles that could be consulted, and astrology was accepted as normal. At the heart of traditional Roman religion was the consultation of the entrails of sacrificial victims to make predictions; and emperors consulted the books of Sibylline oracles before going to war. Justin in his *Apology* makes much of the fulfilment of prophecy – miracles he regards as two-a-penny, and so unconvincing; but the fulfilment of the prophecies in the Jewish scriptures he documents at great length because for him it is the most solid argument. Indeed, when he tells the story of the coming of Logos/Word in Jesus Christ he does it entirely through prophecies drawn from the Jewish scriptures.

Second, this argument reinforced the notion of the providential rule of the one God – the 'monarchy' which oversees everything according to the divine purpose and will. God's plan for the universe and everything in it was laid down in the prophecies inspired by the Holy Spirit.

Third, this perspective ensured that the prophetic books of the Old Testament would stay at the centre of the life of the community, even when New Testament books began to be collected and read as scripture alongside them, and some, like Marcion, challenged the status of the Jewish scriptures. Christian gatherings were around books and their interpretation; to assume that the oracles in these books were riddling and needed to be decoded correctly, by allegory and other methods, was entirely natural, as was their view that the key to interpreting these prophetic books was Christ.

Jesus Christ and the gospel

Besides the detailed discovery of all the ways in which he fulfilled the prophecies, Christ is predominantly presented in second-century literature as the one who reveals the truth about God and teaches the way to live your life. But he is also identified as the King to whom Christians owe absolute loyalty, even unto death, and who will reign when God's kingdom is finally established. Again there are several remarks to be made.

First, there was a running internal battle about the concrete human reality of this Jesus Christ. What people craved was a supernatural visitant; flesh was often denigrated as impure and material, and crucifixion was a disgrace. Some said that the spiritual Christ must have come on Jesus at his baptism and left before the cross, others that he was an angel who only seemed like a human being. Against this we find protests:

> I give glory to Jesus Christ, the God who has made you wise. For I perceive you are fixed in an unshakeable faith, as if nailed body and soul on the cross of the Lord Jesus Christ, rooted in love by his blood, absolutely convinced with respect to our Lord that he was truly of the seed of David as regards the flesh, but by the power and will of God born truly of a virgin, baptized by John that he might fulfil all righteousness and truly nailed in the flesh for our sake under Pontius Pilate and Herod the Tetrarch.[58]

So wrote Ignatius as he was taken across Asia Minor to suffer martyrdom for Christ in the early second century.

Second, the focus on Christ's kingship created a direct challenge to the Ruler-cult, and so was distinctly political in its implications.[59] Honours that Christians gave to Christ mirrored those given to the divine Emperor – he was Lord, King, Son of God, King of kings and Lord of lords, Saviour of the world, the bringer of peace and a golden age. The Hellenistic cities of Asia Minor, Ephesus, Smyrna, Pergamum, have all produced inscriptions and temple remains which bear witness to their rivalry in offering divine honours to the emperor, with processions and festivals; imperial permission for this was greeted as good news (*euangelia*), and as a promise of *sōtēria* (safety or salvation); an imperial state visit was described as an advent or *parousia*, and was greeted with excitement – it would bring largesse, an opportunity for petitions, and other concrete benefits. It was for those cities that the book of Revelation was written, setting up a confrontation with the imperial cult. Christian loyalty was to Christ who would return and establish his kingdom on earth. Around AD 155 Polycarp, Bishop of Smyrna, when captured and invited by the Governor to revile Christ, replied, 'Eighty and six years have I served him, and he has done me no wrong. How then can I blaspheme my King and my Saviour?'[60] The Governor invites him to swear by Caesar's fortune, but this is entirely incompatible with loyalty to Christ, and Polycarp refuses. Even as apologists protested Christian loyalty to the state, there remained an absolute refusal to compromise that loyalty to Christ. In the great persecutions of 250 and 303, that absolute refusal to honour Caesar, or offer incense to the gods that made Rome great, marked out the confessors and martyrs. Christianity had a political edge.

But, third, for both external critics and some internal thinkers, the kingship of Christ was problematic in relation to the monarchy of the one God. In the second and third centuries debates began about the relationship between the one true God, who jealously denied worship to all the gods of the nations, and Christian worship of this man who recently appeared in Palestine. The arguments would go on until after the accession of Constantine, and cannot be explored fully here; but it is interesting to note (i) that the analogy of the emperor sharing his single sovereignty with his son was actually employed in the course of the third-century arguments;[61] and (ii) that the earliest teaching about Christ and his fulfilment of the prophecies does not seem to have posed that theoretical question so explicitly. The one true God acted to fulfil the divine purpose through God's own Word and Spirit, and it was God's own Word that was incarnate in Jesus.

Fourth, the gospel was less about the individual's salvation from personal sin through the atoning sacrifice of Christ and more about the renewal of God's sovereignty over all creation – if only people recognized this and prepared themselves by living in obedience to God's will, waiting for his Son to be revealed from heaven, then there was the promise of a new world order. Those who had been initiated by baptism, dying and rising with Christ, would physically rise from the dead to participate in the kingdom of Christ.

Creation and resurrection

These two ideas were fundamental and closely related to one another.

It seems very likely that the first Christian 'doctrine' to be expressly formulated was the notion of 'creation out of nothing', the argument going like this:[62] the one God could not have made things out of the divine self or everything would be divine; the Creator could not have fashioned things out of pre-existent eternal matter (as the Platonists held) or there would be two eternal first principles (or gods), not one; so God must have brought things into being out of nothing. There was a Greek proverb, 'Nothing comes from nothing' – so Christian philosophers were directly confronting the presuppositions of the culture and challenging them. They were taking on board the philosophical interest in cosmology, and giving it their own twist.

It might be supposed that 'creation out of nothing' was inherited from Judaism, but the primeval chaos of Genesis was easily assimilated to the pre-existent 'matter' of the Platonists, and it is clear that some early Christians and Hellenistic Jews, including Justin, made exactly that move. It was towards the end of the second century that Theophilus, Bishop of Antioch, suggested that if God used pre-existent matter, God was no better than a human craftsman who made things out of wood or stone. 'Creation out of nothing' was grounded in the absolute power and 'monarchy' of the one, living and true God, which was certainly a notion inherited from Judaism and affirmed in the biblical books; but the formulation of this doctrine of creation bespeaks engagement with philosophical questions – the Church was more like a school than a religion as understood in the ancient world.

It is important to emphasize the physicality of the Church's teaching. In the face of heretics who turned resurrection into immortality of the soul, the Church linked it with creation out of nothing.[63] If God can create once, he can create again, and what it is all about is the restoration of what we might call full-bodied life. Even if people have been eaten by wild beasts or drowned and consumed by sea monsters – nothing can impede the power of God to recreate. The Eucharist was called the 'medicine/drug of immortality', and the Christian God was recognized as powerful for guaranteeing life after death. Hence the Christian contempt for death noted earlier. Christ's resurrection was the first-fruits which confirmed the message for those who became his disciples, and prepared themselves for his coming kingdom.

A holy lifestyle

What Jesus came to teach was the holy lifestyle which would make that possible.

To a fair extent, being holy did mean separation: rigorists insisted that converted soldiers had to leave the army because they could not do the equivalent of saluting the flag without being involved in idolatry;[64] so likewise, workers in the theatre or public games, and other professions where contact with paganism could not be avoided.[65] Everyone had to abstain from normal city festivals and social events, because they always involved worship of the gods. It also meant high ethical ideals in daily life. Christians refused to take life – abortion or exposure of unwanted infants, as much as suicide or murder. Furthermore, Christians had to embrace a notion of purity that involved a strict sexual ethic – even pagans like the physician Galen noted this Christian characteristic. Not just fornication and adultery were disapproved, but even second marriage after widowhood; and in a highly influential second-century apocryphal work, Paul is presented as preaching as follows:

> Blessed are the pure in heart, for they shall see God.
> Blessed are they who have kept the flesh pure, for they shall become a temple of God.
> Blessed are the continent, for to them God will speak . . .
> Blessed are they who have wives as if they had them not, for they shall inherit God . . .
> Blessed are they who have kept their baptism secure, for they shall rest with the Father and the Son . . .
> Blessed are the bodies of the virgins, for they shall be well pleasing to God, and shall not lose the reward for their purity.[66]

The story is then told of the betrothed girl, Thekla, who overheard this, refused to marry and followed Paul. Christianity produced such dedicated virgins from its very earliest years, and could be understood as disruptive to normal family life. This may seem extreme, but notice how those beatitudes focus on a future of being in communion with God, and on ensuring that the grace of baptism is not endangered – the resurrection of the body required the avoidance of sin and the purity of the flesh so that it might become a Temple of God.

But all this needs to be put into the context of our opening quotation, with its emphasis on service to others and doing good. Loving God and one's neighbour would remain the essence of Christian holiness, and, as we have seen, however underground the Church seems to have been, it was practical out-workings of those commandments which would prove to be the fundamental way in which Christianity spread.

Conclusion

So, being holy in the cities of the Roman Empire lay at the heart of the Christian mission, and was the core of Christian teaching. The components of that holy lifestyle included abstention from idolatry, from taking life, and from sexual incontinence, while living with 'a single heart' – without duplicity but with honesty, transparency and integrity in all one's dealings.

Postscript

We have considered how and why Christianity spread, and what the content of the message was. I hope this account has indicated something of the extraordinary audacity of this tiny minority community. Their pretensions were absurd, as Celsus noticed in the second century. Here were a

> 'flight of bats or a swarm of ants crawling out of their nest, or frogs in council on a marsh, or worms in synod on a corner of a dunghill, quarrelling as to who is the greatest sinner and declaring that 'God discloses and announces all things to us beforehand . . . God sends messengers to us alone'; or 'there is a God, and next to him are we whom he has made in all points like unto himself, and to whom all things are subject – land and water, air and stars; all things are for our sakes, and are appointed to serve us'; and 'since certain of our number commit sin, God will come or send his Son to burn up the wicked and let the rest of us have life eternal with himself'.[67]

But in those pretensions were the seeds of eventual triumph, as we shall see in the next chapter. There we will explore the situation after the conversion of Constantine, consider the challenge of 'establishment', and ask whether the Christianizing of the Empire facilitated or hampered Christian mission.

Notes

1. Clement 1.2; 2.1–3; ET FY.
2. The classic discussion is found in Adolf Harnack, *The Mission and Expansion of Christianity in the First Three Centuries*, ET James Moffatt, 2 vols, New York: Williams and Norgate, 1908, I, pp. 271 ff.

3. Eusebius, *Church History* IX.9; noted by Martin Goodman, *Mission and Conversion: Proselytizing in the Religious History of the Roman Empire*, Oxford: Clarendon, 1994.

4. On the imperial cult, see S. R. F. Price, *Rituals and Power: The Roman Imperial Cult in Asia Minor*, Cambridge: Cambridge University Press, 1984.

5. Rodney Stark, *The Rise of Christianity: A Sociologist Reconsiders History*, Princeton, NJ: Princeton University Press, 1996, p. 150.

6. Stark (1996), p. 158.

7. Goodman (1994); John J. Collins, *Between Athens and Jerusalem: Jewish Identity in the Hellenistic Diaspora*, second edition, Grand Rapids, MI: Eerdmans, 2000.

8. *Adversus Haereses* I.2.

9. *Contra Celsum* III.9.

10. Eusebius, *Church History* II.3; ET G. A. Williamson, Harmondsworth: Penguin, 1965.

11. Ramsay MacMullen, *Christianizing the Roman Empire AD 100–400*, New Haven and London: Yale University Press, 1984, following Harnack (1908).

12. *Contra Celsum* III.9; ET Henry Chadwick, Cambridge: Cambridge University Press, 1965.

13. As noted by Harnack (1908), I, p. 86; MacMullen (1984), pp. 33–4; Goodman (1994), pp. 106–8.

14. MacMullen (1984), pp. 34–5, quoting Origen, *Contra Celsum* VIII.69 and Minucius Felix VIII.4.

15. For example *Didache*.

16. Lucian, *Peregrinus*.

17. Stephen Benko, *Pagan Rome and the Early Christians*, London: Batsford, 1984, pp. 45 ff.

18. MacMullen (1984), pp. 59–61.

19. MacMullen (1984), Chapter 4.

20. Harnack (1908), I, p. 131.

21. *Contra Celsum* I.46, 67; II.49.

22. Benko (1984), pp. 113–14, quoting Lactantius, *De Morte Persecutorum* 10.

23. Athanasius, *Life of Antony* 74–80.

24. Eusebius, *Martyrs of Palestine* 4.14.

25. For example Origen. *Contra Celsum* I.6, II.49; VI.39, VII.36; VIII.60; cf. Benko (1984), Chapter VI.

26. For example *Contra Celsum* I.6; VII.4.

27. MacMullen (1984).

28. Harnack (1908), II, pp. 335–6, quoted by Stark (1996), p. 14.

29. Stark (1996), Chapter 1. Of course estimates of population are hazardous given the kind of evidence available, but there have been good reasons for suggesting that around the time of the final intense persecutions (from 303 until Constantine's victories) the Christian population had reached

around 10 per cent of the Empire's total. Stark's Table (p. 7) shows that at the same rate of expansion it would have been more than half 50 years later (that is even without Constantine's conversion); while the previous 50 years would have seen an increase from 1 per cent to that 10 per cent, which would be enough to account for the impression of huge increase in the second half of the third century.

30. *Epistle to Diognetus* 5–6; ET Andrew Louth, *Early Christian Writings*, London: Penguin, 1987, modified.
31. Origen, *Contra Celsum* I.1,7, VIII.20; III.55.
32. Harnack (1908), II, pp. 64 ff, documents the importance of women and women martyrs in the early Church, a point frequently reiterated in the literature.
33. Harnack (1908), I, pp. 371–2.
34. For Rome, see Peter Lampe, *From Paul to Valentinus*, London: T & T Clark, 2003.
35. Eusebius, *Church History* 6.43.
36. *Apology* 39.
37. Harnack (1908), I, p. 176.
38. Harnack (1908), I, pp. 177 ff.
39. Benko (1984), p. 141.
40. See Stark (1996), Chapter 4.
41. Eusebius, *Church History* 7.22.
42. *Apology* 39.
43. *Mortality* 15–20.
44. Benko (1984), pp. 39–40, citing Lucian, *De Morte Peregrini* 13.
45. Harnack (1908), I, pp. 112–13 for a few examples.
46. Goodman (1994).
47. See for example Louis H. Feldman, *Jew and Gentile in the Ancient World*, Princeton: Princeton University Press 1993.
48. Goodman (1994), p. 120.
49. Goodman (1994), pp. 96–7.
50. Origen, *Contra Celsum* VIII.38.
51. See Markus Vinzent, 'Rome' in *The Cambridge History of Christianity: Origins to Constantine*, Cambridge: Cambridge University Press, 2006, summarizing the detailed research of Lampe (2003). Other teachers who fit the description include some later rejected as heretical: Valentinus, Marcion, etc.
52. L. Michael White, *Building God's House in the Roman World*, Baltimore and London: John Hopkins University Press, 1990, p. 110.
53. For example *Epistle to Diognetus* 5.
54. For example *Contra Celsum* II.30; later Eusebius takes this for granted.
55. Robert Grant, *Early Christianity and Society*, London: Collins, 1978, Chapter 2.
56. 1 Clement 21.3.8–9; ET FY.

57. Ignatius, *Ephesians* 15.3; ET FY.

58. Ignatius, *Smyrnaeans* 1; ET FY.

59. See Allen Brent, *A Political History of Early Christianity*, London: T & T Clark, 2009; Frances Young, 'Christianity' in Christopher Rowe and Malcolm Schofield (eds), *The Cambridge History of Greek and Roman Political Thought*, Cambridge: Cambridge University Press, 2000.

60. *Martyrdom of Polycarp* 9; ET Maxwell Stanforth in *Early Christian Writings*, Harmondsworth: Penguin 1968; rev. edn Andrew Louth (ed.), 1987.

61. Tertullian, *Adversus Praxeam*.

62. Tertullian, *Adversus Hermogenem*. For further discussion see my article, '"Creatio ex nihilo": A Context for the Emergence of the Christian Doctrine of Creation' in *Scottish Journal of Theology* 44 (1991), pp. 139–51.

63. For further discussion see my paper, 'Naked or Clothed? Eschatology and the Doctrine of Creation' in Peter Clarke and Tony Claydon (eds), *The Church, the Afterlife and the Fate of the Soul*, Studies in Church History 45, Woodbridge, Suffolk: Boydell and Brewer, 2009.

64. However, Harnack (1908), II, pp. 52 ff details the large number of soldiers known to have converted without leaving the army.

65. Tertullian in *De Idolatria* 8 lists as people who had to be especially careful carpenters, workers in stucco, joiners, slaters, workers in gold leaf, painters, brass-workers and engravers – any of them could be employed in the manufacture of idols or things needed for idol-worship; astrologers and magicians, schoolmasters, usurers, holders of civic office, and anyone trading in incense were not to continue to practise. Harnack (1908), I, p. 305.

66. *Acts of Paul and Thekla* 5–6; ET in R. McL. Wilson (ed.), ET of E. Hennecke, *New Testament Apocrypha*, vol. II 'Apostolic and Early Church Writings', London: Lutterworth 1965, p. 354.

67. *Contra Celsum* IV.23; quoted from Harnack (1908), I, p. 242.

4

The Challenge of Establishment–Did a Christian Empire Help or Hinder?

FRANCES YOUNG

So far we have discovered that

- Christianity spread through networks of contacts and the creation of loving supportive communities, on the basis of a reputation for access to divine power and miracle, a remarkable sexual continence and disregard of death;
- those attracted would join a school-like household where they learned about the monarchy of the one God, the reality of God's creation, providence and oversight of everything, even the secrets of the heart – truths which offered citizenship of another realm and demanded the strictest lifestyle, the rejection of idolatry and undeviating loyalty even unto death, following the example of God's Son, whose life, teaching, death and resurrection were for the sake of revealing the truth and opening the way to resurrection into God's kingdom;
- keeping themselves to themselves and always in danger of being informed against to the authorities, the churches nevertheless grew.

So it is generally reckoned that by the end of the third century Christians constituted 10 per cent of the population, based mainly in the cities, but now owning property, meeting in buildings converted for church use and often led by prominent citizens, despite their withdrawal from much communal life on the grounds that it was steeped in idolatrous practices. For half a century there had been relative peace; but then in 303, faced with various economic and military challenges, the Emperor Diocletian sought restoration of Rome's greatness and decided the entire Empire should unite in worshipping the gods which had traditionally preserved the Empire and the universe from catastrophe. Christians were suspected of disloyalty and soon the last terrible Empire-wide persecution was under way, only to be dramatically followed by a complete reversal of policy with the conversion of Constantine, who believed he was victorious through the power of the Christian God.[1] The character of the Constantinian revolution, together with its consequences for the mission of the Church, is the subject of this chapter.

The religion of the emperors

Constantine's religion has been repeatedly debated: was he or was he not a Christian? In many ways his religion remained what it was.[2] Like most people in the ancient world he looked for the benefits brought by the gods. Apollo, the sun-god, had been his patron as he moved towards a kind of pagan monotheism. His allegiance to Apollo had been a response to a dream, and on the eve of battle in 312 he is said to have had a vision of the cross over the sun, interpreted by another dream and a voice: 'In this sign conquer.' The God who thus appeared to him brought victory, so now as Emperor of the West he offered patronage to that God's priests and worshippers, a course whose rightness was confirmed by the awful fates of the emperors who had persecuted Christians. Religion was associated with power; success was proof.

So Constantine's conversion experience was not the sort of thing expected by evangelicals, nor was the establishment of the Church under Constantine the sort of establishment we have known in later European history. Constantine's coin-issues, which were a form of propaganda in the ancient world, indicate that for some time to come he allowed his mints to continue honouring the old gods (one shows Jupiter rather than the God of the Christians handing over Victory to Constantine) – indeed, coins show the sun-god in particular, whose festival date was 25 December and whose iconography was at the time being adapted to depict Christ! There is a famous painting in a Christian tomb under the Vatican showing Christ as the sun-god riding his chariot across the sky.[3] So ambiguity was in the air, and indeed the sign that Constantine had painted on the shields of his legionaries is itself ambiguous: the Chi-Rho sign is not the cross as we know it, and even though interpreted as the initial letters (in Greek) of the name 'Christ', might in some forms of it appear to symbolize the sun with a cross below it.[4]

There was no clean sweep – it would hardly have been possible to change the whole culture overnight. Pagans would continue in high imperial office and at the head of the army for well over a century. Constantine did apparently refuse to sacrifice to the gods on arrival in Rome, though as Emperor he certainly carried out other imperial rituals, despite its pagan connotations. He is said to have legislated against sacrifice, but later emperors were still trying to suppress it.[5] He did legislate against crucifixion and would eventually try to impose strict marriage laws in accordance with Christian sexual ethics, forbidding concubinage and divorce. But there was no clean sweep – he had to keep the majority of his subjects on his side, after all. However, there was patronage, and this would have increasing impacts, especially as it was extended to the East with Constantine's subsequent triumphant reunification of the whole Empire.

So how did Constantine patronize the Church?[6] To start with, he brought persecution to an end and demanded that all properties be restored to the churches, or if that were now impossible, compensation be made. Then he exempted clergy from civil duties and church lands from taxes, while allowing bishops to travel in the imperial post on Church business. Where previous emperors had presented cities with temples, supported priesthoods and subsidized religious festivals and feasts, Constantine enriched the Church with an extraordinary number of enormous grand basilicas, in Rome, Trier, Antioch, Jerusalem and Constantinople, his new Eastern capital.

Provincial officials were ordered to provide labour and material. Grain allowances were made for the virgins, widows and others dependent on the churches. Imperial support for pagan rites and temples was discontinued, and their treasuries plundered for public use.[7] Local elites soon followed the Emperor in glorifying their local city by giving gifts to the local church rather than the one-time powerhouses of pagan religion, so that by the time of Julian, the apostate Emperor who tried to put the clock back and reinstate paganism in the early 360s, it was already difficult because of the decline enforced by deprivation of funds.

As a result there were significant power shifts in urban society. Churches had been endowed with land and wealth, which meant ecclesiastical agents began to manage property, and economic power began to shift into the hands of the bishop. To some extent the Church's local organization had long been modelled on municipal structures, but local magistracies and priesthoods had always rotated around the leading families, whereas ordination to the Church's priesthood was for life, as was a bishop's appointment to his see, so concentrating local power and influence.[8] The material benefits of belonging to the Church soon led to various kinds of abuse or corruption, bishoprics being bought, and Church property diverted for personal use.[9] The power accruing to bishops led to careerism, and even the election of the local magnate whether or not he was a committed Christian. A case in point is Synesius of Cyrene,[10] a local dignitary who at the end of the century, having acted as an envoy to the imperial court on behalf of his own city, became bishop of a nearby city by popular demand, despite indicating to the patriarch that he would be prepared to promulgate myths in the pulpit if permitted to practise philosophy in private: his Neoplatonic Trinity and Christian doctrine merged into a single mystical conception celebrated in his poetry. Was he really a Christian at all? – the very question asked about Constantine himself!

Meanwhile, however, it is just possible that we have available a speech given by Constantine himself which reveals something of his thinking. Probably within a year or two of his victory in the West the Emperor addressed an assembly of clergy in Rome in a Latin speech known as *The Oration of the Saints*, preserved only in Greek translation. Almost everything in that last sentence has been disputed: the authenticity, the date and even the original language of the speech. But enough of a consensus is gathering for us to have some confidence that, even if Constantine employed a bishop as speech-writer, we can still hear Constantine attempting a definition of his own relationship with the Church,[11] and the mission of God within which he and the Church had a role to play.

The occasion was the anniversary of the Passion – this we know from the opening words, celebrating the coming of light, the prelude to the resurrection, the day of affliction. That Constantine chose Good Friday is highly significant – he 'would seem to have been the first Christian who could trace his faith directly to a vision of the Cross'.[12] Up to the time of Constantine the cross is never found in Christian art, but the story of Constantine's conversion focused on the sign of the cross over the sun; and it is from now on that the cross does begin to appear in Christian art. Soon the legend of the finding of the true cross by Helena, Constantine's mother, would gain widespread currency. Constantine saw the cross as the saving symbol, or the instrument of God's victory.

The elites in Rome would certainly have been suspicious of Constantine, both as a usurper and as a patron of the Church. He may well have needed to explain himself to a variety of audiences. Here he is respectful to the gathered clergy, asks for their aid and correction, yet offers the testimony of a convert: in effect he says, 'Would to God I had been given this revelation long since', rehearsing apologetic arguments for the faith he has adopted. The speech would have lasted approximately two hours and covers three topics: the case for monotheism over against a plurality of gods, the incarnation of the Son of God, and his own reliance on Christ, by contrast with his predecessors, the persecutors. There are some important unifying themes. One, implicit if not fully explicit, is the link between monotheism and monarchy. There needs to be a single sovereignty over creation, otherwise there would be chaos among the elements and harmony would be destroyed by jealousy and ambition. The fact that there is a universal order is proof that everything is under the providential care of one superior power – discord among heavenly powers would produce confusion on earth. This argument undergirds attacks on polytheism, the myths of the gods, idolatry and philosophies based on chance and fate. Implied here perhaps is Constantine's ambition, soon to be fulfilled, to be the sole ruler of a reunited Empire, the monarch on earth imaging the monarch of all, according to God's special dispensation. A fundamental element in Constantine's policy was to establish unity, and repeatedly he tried to impose unity on a disunited Church. His aim was one Church, one faith, one Empire under the one God, whose providence had brought him, Constantine, to power in order to achieve this as the one Emperor.

A second overarching theme concerns proper worship of the true God, and this is not by sacrifice, against which Constantine rails in a long aside. He repeatedly indicates that proper worship is by prayerful devotion, thanksgivings and living a righteous and holy life. The Saviour founded the Church as a 'holy temple of virtue, an immortal, imperishable temple wherein the worship due to the Supreme Father and himself (that is the Saviour) is piously performed'. For Constantine this virtue is what makes Christianity superior:

> With us isn't there genuine concord and unwearied love of others? . . . Don't we exercise faith towards God and also fidelity in social relationships? Don't we pity the unfortunate? Isn't our life one of simplicity, without fraud or hypocrisy? Don't we acknowledge the true God and his undivided sovereignty? This is true godliness, religion sincere and undefiled, the life of wisdom, and those who have it are travellers on a noble road leading to eternal life. We cannot doubt that the Deity is pleased with excellence in human conduct.[13]

This is the kind of thing Constantine asserts, firmly conjoining ethics and religion in a way unknown in paganism but at the heart of the biblical tradition, and given warrant by reference to God's oversight of our lives, with consequent reward or punishment in due course. The universe is morally ordered and subject to God's providence.

If this speech is anything to go by, Constantine's grasp of Christian theology went well beyond mere monotheism, despite the arguments of some scholars. He asks for the inspiration of the Spirit of the Father and Son, and affirms that the transcendent, ultimate God works through the Logos/Word, the pre-existent Son of God, to whom is delegated cosmic oversight, both as creator and as risen and ascended king in heaven – the one eventually to be depicted in gilded mosaic images of the Pantocrator (Almighty), high above the heads of worshippers in the central dome of Eastern Ortho-dox churches. It was this Son of God who in his benevolence and *philanthropia* (love of humankind) became incarnate. Constantine knows about the virgin birth, the baptism, miracles, teaching, heal-ings; he alludes specifically to the feeding of the 5,000 and the still-ing of the storm, speaks of the Son of God visiting the sick, relieving afflictions and consoling the poor, and refers to Peter's sword when reporting on how Christ taught contempt of danger by example and rebuked aggressive retaliation – this, he says, is heavenly wis-dom: to endure rather than to inflict injury. More than once he focuses on the cross as a demonstration of God's determination to deal with iniquity and establish order and justice, or of Christ's victory over sin. God's gracious kindness is a repeated theme. He guarantees the truth of it all by appeal to the fulfilment of prophecy – referring not only to the biblical material but also to the Sibylline Oracles and Virgil. In other words, Constantine has learned from the long tradition of Christian apologetic writings, even suggesting, as they did, that despite the wrong-headedness of the philosophers meddling with things beyond understanding, Plato did get an ink-ling of the truth.

Power, victory, success, unity – these are Constantine's dominant interests and dominant themes. His confidence in God will be rati-fied soon by another victory over his Eastern rival. *God's mission is identified with Constantine's mission.* Christ is his invincible ally, protector of the righteous, supreme judge and giver of everlasting life. The Emperor, even if he now repudiates divinity for himself and acknowledges his own mortality, remains a key instrument of God's purpose on earth. So both in this speech and in other documents preserved for us by Eusebius, the contemporary bishop of Caesarea in Palestine, we find Constantine appealing to people to embrace the truth. The seeds of Christendom are beginning to germinate, and within a couple of generations there will be laws against pagans, Jews and heretics. Constantine himself claimed to be the bishop for those outside the Church, but seems to have been increasingly intolerant of non-conformity, and sooner or later social expediency, material reward and coercion would become signifi-cant factors in the Church's expansion.[14] The big question then is whether Christianity lost its soul in the process. It is time to look at the Church's reaction.

The Church's response – continuities and discontinuities

A sense of unexpected fulfilment

The Eusebius of Caesarea just mentioned is known as the first historian of the Church. His monumental work, the ten books of his *Church History*, went through various editions, with extra books keeping it up to date. It is possible that the earliest edition was produced before Constantine appeared on the scene. In fact by the time Constantine conquered in the East, where persecution had rumbled on for another ten years, Eusebius was already 50. Yet he outlived the first Christian Emperor, and compiled a *Life of Constantine*,[15] which is a major source for historians, though problematic insofar as it is a celebration in the mould of ancient praise-speeches, full of spin and suppressing uncomfortable facts: Eusebius states he is only concerned to present 'those royal and noble actions which are pleasing to God, the Sovereign of all'[16] because it would be disgraceful if the evil deeds of a Nero were given fine rhetorical treatment, while Constantine's goodness was passed over in silence. But true to his usual compositional method, Eusebius preserves important texts, quoting them at length – Constantine's *Oration to the Saints* is one of these. So what did Eusebius, a venerable bishop of the time, think about Constantine?

First and foremost, Constantine had come as the final proof of God's providential activity in history. Eusebius' thought is in direct continuity with the emphasis on God's monarchy in the last chapter, but with the fulfilment of God's purposes now possible through the earthly monarchy of Constantine. The empire on earth is an imitation of God's sovereign rule in heaven; so there is one God and one emperor under God. Monarchy alone ensures peace – democracy means anarchy. But with Constantine's advent, the wicked have been judged, evil and idolatry are overcome; peace has been established both in the world and in the Church. Constantine reflects Christ the teacher, becoming the ideal philosopher-king, who has the right to rule others because he has learned to govern his own unruly passions (a typical motif of imperial encomium and barely Christianized);[17] but this means he refuses excess flattery, cares nothing for his gorgeous apparel, the paraphernalia of his office or the sheer power of his position, but rather displays the Christian virtues of humility, generosity and piety. Direct communication with God's Logos/Word is attributed to him; so that he becomes a teacher and example to his subjects, illuminating them in the most distant corners of the Empire, like the sun. For the bishops to feast with Constantine is like feasting in the kingdom of God. Eusebius endorses to the hilt the policies of Constantine – the desire for peace and unity in Empire and Church, the assertion of the truth of Christianity over against polytheism, the association of monarchy and monotheism. He even gave in to Constantine on a matter of doctrine, agreeing to the proposed creed at the Council of Nicaea and then writing a rather embarrassed letter of explanation to his congregation.

Eusebius was not alone in celebrating what seemed like the fulfilment of God's mission on earth, namely, the conversion of society to Christianity – he is just a very good example, not least because we have so much of his writing. A century or so later his church history was continued by someone called Socrates. He thought Eusebius' treatment of Constantine was more rhetorical than an accurate statement of the facts, so his first book covers Constantine's reign, and then continues up to more or less his own day. Where Eusebius had contrasted his history with the classics, on the grounds that they were all about wars whereas he focused on the peace of the Church, Socrates thinks conflict is the subject-matter of history, and sees disputes in the Church as integrally linked with the Empire's wars. [18] He has become almost cynical about ecclesiastics and ecclesiastical politics, and claims that his subject is the 'contentious disputes of bishops and their insidious designs against one another'. He had reason for this changed perspective.

The struggle for unity

Constantine thought that favouring the Church would help towards the unity of the Empire, but the first thing Constantine found himself doing after his victory in the West was trying to settle a division in the Church in North Africa. In a dispute arising out of the persecution, both sides appealed to him to settle their differences. A Church council was called to meet in the Emperor's presence; there were many precedents for councils of bishops, and even for a Church appeal to the Emperor, but the Emperor himself had not as yet facilitated a

Church council – it would become a habit! The Church had always struggled for unity, as the New Testament itself shows; and, generally speaking, disagreement led to excommunication, to schism, to mutual condemnation as heretical: 'One, holy, catholic and apostolic' was achieved by exclusion. This could be on the grounds of false teaching, or conduct that did not conform to Christian ethical norms, or simply dissension, which was, of course, not Christian in any case!

Constantine struggled for Church unity, finding more intractable problems in the East. The Council of Nicaea in 325 was supposed to sort those out, but no settlement was achieved, controversy rumbling on till nearly the end of the century, with shifting alliances and constant attempts at compromise. In the East, both Constantine and his successors favoured the party which seemed to control the majority of bishoprics and the most powerful sees, while exiling those who seemed like trouble-makers. From the standpoint of later historians like Socrates, this meant the 'orthodox' had been suppressed, and their story was the struggle of heroes like Athanasius against the so-called 'Arian' party, which was long in the ascendant. Socrates may well have been writing to celebrate the unity of Empire and Church under Theodosius II, the Emperor of his own day, just as Eusebius had prematurely celebrated Constantine's achievement. In the long run, Eusebius had supported the wrong side, and his reputation for being an Arian clouded his legacy. So can we identify the so-called 'orthodox' as a kind of resistance movement, conscientiously objecting to the imperial captivity of the Church? Hardly – all sides sought to get their heroes recalled from exile and recognized as legitimate bishops and the truth, as they saw it, accepted in councils called by the emperors. It was the advent in the East of a new Emperor from the West, Theodosius I, which led to the so-called triumph of Nicene orthodoxy in 381.

Now it would be easy to get distracted into the long story of doctrinal conflict and the way this was affected by the involvement of the Emperors in Church affairs. But I shall simply make three comments:

- The doctrinal struggles of these centuries tend to be presented in hindsight as 'binary oppositions' – straightforward battles between orthodoxy on the one hand and heresy on the other. However, recent scholarship has shown how much more complicated it all was, with shifting alliances as bishops in one council after another tried to express the truth about God, and about Jesus Christ as the incarnate Son of God. [19] The doctrines of the Trinity and of Christology were being forged through this historical process, with many of the arguments deriving from differing exegeses of key scriptural passages. Meanwhile emperors sat at the touchlines, or tried to act as referees, or even attempted to force compromise solutions on the bishops, constantly frustrated that unity was so elusive.

- For 50 years a hierarchical understanding was dominant: the transcendent God was mediated to the creation through the Logos (Word), who was 'like God' and God's representative, but not 'of one substance with the Father'. It could be argued that this view matched the social reality of earthly monarchy and delegated powers. It was a convenient doctrine supporting Eusebius' affirmation of the monarchy of God and of Constantine. The orthodox resistance was more counter-cultural, arguing in the end that both the Logos and the Holy Spirit must be truly God, since only God could save and sanctify humanity, restoring the image and likeness of God to all humankind. There is only one God, but that one God is Trinity.

- Mission beyond the Roman frontiers was affected by these controversies; for example, Ulfilas, the Bishop of the Goths, was converted when the so-called semi-Arians dominated the Eastern capital. Later the Goths invaded the Western Empire, and Western Christians found themselves subservient to rulers they regarded as heretical. Nevertheless, at least one Christian account of the fall of Rome to the Goths in 410 suggested that their conversion and consequent respect for the Apostle Peter was the reason for the fact that the church over his tomb was respected as an asylum.[20]

Grasping opportunities for Christianization

Given the basic outlook of Christians, taught by the Church the kind of things outlined in the previous chapter, it should come as no surprise that the opportunity to convert all their fellow-citizens and neighbours to the truth was welcomed and exploited. Clearly it was the mission of God that through the Church all should come to recognize the one God, whose love for humanity was shown in the incarnation, death and resurrection of Jesus Christ, through whom life and salvation would be granted to all who believe and live a pure and holy life. But the process of converting society was bound to involve ambiguities, the Church itself being changed by having to take on the ancient roles of religion expected in Late Antiquity.

Constantine's huge building programme left its mark. The landscape of key cities was changed – indeed, not just the landscape but the very perception of what a religious building was for. Most of the religions around the Mediterranean built temples or shrines which were dwelling-places for the gods, housing their images. Many temples, especially in Egypt and the Middle East, denied access to the crowds of worshippers – only priests entered to minister to the god's needs, and sacrifices were offered in courts outside. Images occasionally appeared; often in cities around the Mediterranean they were processed through the streets at festivals, with dancing, excitements, feasts and communal jollification. By contrast, for Christians, human bodies were temples of the Holy Spirit and human persons were images of God. Having gathered for worship in houses, they now built basilicas, public gathering-spaces. 'Basilica' means 'king's hall'; basilicas had been built by emperors in cities as centres for imperial and public business – here lawsuits would be pursued, taxes exacted and commerce pursued, while orators and philosophers would have taken advantage of the space to promulgate their views. Now the term came to signify the hall of Christ the King. People came to hear speeches in his honour, homilies based on God's Word, the scriptures. The kind of rhetoric used in civic basilicas was adapted for use in religious basilicas, and by the end of the century people flocked to Christian basilicas for entertainment – John Chrysostom, nicknamed the 'Goldenmouth',[21] lets us have glimpses of this as he warns his hearers of potential pick-pockets, tells them off for applauding, but still exploits rhetorical tricks, including images from the theatre, to catch attention. Yet his preaching and that of others was a struggle to wean people off the theatre – it was too contaminated with paganism and immorality, indeed, to change their entire way of life. The preaching was both encultured, using the rhetorical tricks of the age, and also counter-cultural.

In these vast spaces, churches began to enact processions and displays, their officials decked out in rich robes, with the biblical stories depicted in murals and mosaics where civic basilicas would have been decorated with classical myths. A profound cultural transformation was beginning, with new stories and histories replacing the old traditional ones. But change went both ways: liturgical developments accompanied the architectural developments, not least because of the huge numbers of people beginning to flock to the churches rather than the pagan temples. Most people in the crowds remained catechumens, uninitiated, half-committed – baptism was increasingly put off for fear of being contaminated with sin by life in the world; Constantine himself only received baptism on his death-bed. The sacrament of communion was reserved for those baptized, and long since had assimilated features of the 'mystery-religions'; eventually in Eastern Orthodoxy it would become a mystery celebrated behind the screen of the iconostasis. So most people were there only for the service of the Word – the reading of scripture and its interpretation; only the select few remained for the sacrament. Christian standards were constantly preached, but increasingly the majority felt unable to live up to them. Only the really committed were baptized.

By the end of the century, confrontation with paganism was increasingly encouraged by the imperial authorities, and we find vivid accounts of how, in Alexandria and elsewhere, there were street battles between Christians and pagans, pagan temples were destroyed, the daemons exorcized, and the sites taken over for Christian use – thus displaying the power of the Christian God over against other gods.[22] In Alexandria the images were melted down to make useful pots for the poor, except for one idol, which was set up in a public place in order that the whole idea of images of the gods could be mocked. The taking over of sacred sites can still be experienced by tourists: the Pantheon in Rome is an ancient Roman building dedicated to all the gods (which is what Pantheon means), and it still stands because it was converted into a church; and the interior of the medieval cathedral in Syracuse turns out to be a Greek temple. We know that the destruction of the Serapeum in Alexandria (the temple complex of the god Sarapis) meant that the site was converted into a church and became the bishop's headquarters.[23]

The taking over of the Serapeum in Alexandria had another outcome – the adoption of the ancient hieroglyphic sign for 'life', the *ankh*, as the Egyptian Christian sign of the cross.[24] Another apparent take-over is found in icons of the Galaktrophousa – the Virgin feeding milk to the child from her breast, as the Goddess Isis had fed Osiris.[25] This process of taking over and baptizing into Christ effected enculturation, but also changed the Church. A battle over pictures and images is evident all through the fourth century. Eusebius mentions portraits of Paul, Peter and Christ he has seen, along with a bronze statue of a kneeling woman, facing the figure of a man with his hand outstretched, supposedly Jesus and the woman with a haemorrhage – indeed he claims that they stood outside her house at Paneas near Caesarea Philippi, but comments that Gentile custom underlay this.[26] At the end of the century, Bishop Epiphanius tells how he went into a church to pray and, finding an embroidered curtain hanging on the doors with an image of Christ or one of the saints, tore it apart – for him any image in church was tantamount to idolatry and contrary to the teaching of the scriptures.[27] Later, under the Byzantines, iconoclasts would have the same kind of destructive impact as the Puritans in England; they were ultimately overcome, but it is worth noting that the Church in the East has never allowed carved images or statues, only icons – the now well-known painted pictures of Eastern Orthodoxy.

This enculturation had further impacts: according to a legend that emerges during the fourth century, Helena, Constantine's mother, when visiting the Holy Land, found the true cross and the nails which fixed the body of Christ to the wood.[28] Soon bits of the true cross were being distributed all over the place, and the development of interest in relics had begun. The nails, they said, were turned into a helmet and bridle bits for her son, the emperor – in other words they were to function as an amulet or talisman to protect him. Powerful biblical names had long been exploited by magicians, and now magical and powerful relics with Christian associations were replacing older pagan charms. Christianity, perforce, had to provide what the old religions had, however superstitious. But it also put such things in a different kind of context. Helena, we are told, took soil from the Holy Land back to Rome, so that she could pray on earth where the feet of the incarnate God had trod; in Palestine, shrines and churches increasingly marked the location of key Gospel narratives, and pilgrimage began to take off. Some protested that Christ could be found anywhere, and journeying to the Holy Land was unnecessary. Yet these developments attest the growing sense that because of the incarnation you could be in physical contact with the divine. Christianization did introduce a new, characteristically Christian aspect to those old habits and mentalities.

It is in this perspective, too, that we must view the increasing cult of the saints. Pagans honoured the dead with dinner-parties at their tombs, and Christians had celebrated the Eucharist in catacombs long before Constantine, so memorializing martyrs and saints. Now people came to local saints to ask for their prayers, making offerings at martyr-shrines and celebrating saints' days; and some of these saints even seem to have been 'baptized' local deities. In the early fifth century an apologist had to explain that this was not a reinstatement of polytheism – saints and martyrs were holy men and women who could mediate with Christ and with God the Father.[29] It is also in this period we begin to find legends about the 'dormition' of Mary and her assumption into heaven, with relics circulating and shrines which claimed to be her tomb – gradually the cult of the Virgin-mother begins to replace the virgin-mother goddesses of fertility in paganism.[30] One heresy-hunter condemned groups where women were acting as priestesses and offering devotion to the Virgin, and warned against treating her as a goddess.[31] Yet alongside this is increasing emphasis on her indispensable role in the incarnation – the reality of her humanity and her giving of humanity to Christ, the new Adam, and also her parallel to Eve, ensuring salvation for the whole human race. In other words the cultural influences went both ways. She came to be honoured as *Theotokos* – the 'birth-giver' of God, the one who had willingly co-operated with God in the incarnation. However much pagan habits of thought, as well as pagan holy sites and practices, were adopted into Christianity, there was also a genuine process of baptizing into Christ – of Christianization – of continuities and discontinuities.

Resistance?

Was there, then, any serious resistance to a process which could be seen as the world taking over the Church? We have noted that some struggled with the fact that the emperor supported their doctrinal opponents, but despite these ambiguities, they still looked for the triumph of their version of Christianity through the support of the imperial authorities. Most thought that the secular power should suppress heretics, as well as pagans and Jews, and few objected to violence to accomplish this. But it is perhaps significant that the rise of the monastic movement coincides with the reign of Constantine and his immediate successors. Were the monks the true guardians of the flame as the Church increasingly conformed to the world?

It is certainly true that the monks saw themselves as inheriting the mantle of the martyrs.[32] Where the martyrs had fought with the daemons and continued Christ's struggle with the devil, confident in victory over sin and death because of Christ's resurrection, the monks went off into the desert to struggle with temptation, to keep themselves pure of sin, to become like God and restore Paradise, a motif found in legends of their miraculous, peaceful relationship with lions and other wild beasts. They sought to live the Christian life at the highest possible standards, to become like God, to be holy, overcoming the cravings and desires of the flesh so as to be 'passionless', to live a life of constant prayer, working with their hands to earn enough to support a fundamentally simple life. They withdrew from the world to avoid the demands, temptations and corruptions of society and business – in other words, they separated themselves quite literally from the world and the worldly Church: there are many stories of tensions between bishops and monks, the ecclesiastical authorities being seen by the monks to compromise with the world, and the monks being far too independent for their bishops' liking. However, a simple picture of monastic resistance to what was happening to the Church under Christian emperors is hardly true to all the evidence. We need to look a bit more closely at this movement:

• It was not as new as all that. Christians had long practised asceticism – there had been, in most churches, from an early date, groups of dedicated virgins, women who refused marriage, and widows who refused second marriage; individual men too would dedicate themselves to a life of fasting and sexual abstinence. From the beginning, Christianity had a strict sexual ethic and practised fasting. The new element was the decision to go into the desert, away from human settlements;

and yet monks were never that far away, and it is now recognized that in many parts of the Empire urban monasteries rapidly grew up.

• It would not be long before men took up the monastic life with enthusiasm in their youth, and then became leading bishops – Basil of Caesarea, John Chrysostom, and Augustine are just a few of the most well-known examples. The desert and the city were not that separate.

• The monks were the shock-troops in the fight against paganism, often invading the cities and leading mob attacks on temples. They were fanatics, but their extremism supported the policies of Church and Empire.

• Famous monks, notably the pillar saints, became heroes of the faith, holy men sought by crowds because of their reputation for miraculous powers and healings; they brought about mass conversions as a result, and were even consulted like oracles by the emperors.

In other words, monks and ascetics were at the forefront of the Christianization process. They were implicated in the ambiguities of a society undergoing religious change. They were not simply a heroic resistance movement trying to hang on to the old radical commitments of the pre-Constantinian Church.

The message preached

After all this, we might be tempted to think that the post-Constantinian Church was largely concerned with success, power, unity, uniformity and doctrinal truth, thus mirroring the interests of the emperors and providing what ancient peoples thought religion should provide. And yes, we would be right, up to a point. But let's turn to examples of the content of the preaching delivered to the vast, semi-Christian crowds which were now flocking to impressive basilicas.

Much preaching remained exegetical – the reading and exposition of scripture was the main thing the crowds would experience. They were being introduced to a new literature, a new set of stories, a new history, to replace the old myths and legends of the traditional cultures comprising the Roman Empire; and this re-education was facilitated both by constant reference to key scriptural narratives and key biblical characters as examples, and also by the rapid development of Christian art – frescoes or mosaics on the walls and roofs of the basilicas told the stories visually.

Some preaching expounded or argued for particular doctrines, especially during the intense controversies that beset the Church, as the pressure for unity and uniformity continued. But another reason for taking themes arose from the Church's calendar, the festivals that had been traditional (Epiphany, the Lent fast, Easter), and as liturgy developed further new festivals (Christmas, Holy Week), not to mention the celebration of saints' days. Some themes were topical, dealing with current catastrophes in a pastoral way: John Chrysostom, regarded as the greatest preacher of the ancient world, preached a series of sermons in Antioch interpreting recent terrible events, when in protest against taxes the citizens had rioted and smashed all the imperial statues – everyone was terrified of reprisals. The majority of sermons were ethical, endeavouring to Christianize the behaviour of notionally Christian crowds. Repentance and the folly of seeking earthly glory, the endeavour to live a holy life, being sanctified so as to become like God – all these were important themes.

A surprising number were on care for the poor.[33] For centuries citizens, particularly the elite, had been expected to expend their wealth to benefit the city, providing for public works, funding theatres, fountains and festivals, subsidizing education and food doles for the community. However, the destitute were generally excluded – the poor with connections might be able to pull strings to get patronage, but generally beggars did not belong. Christians, like Jews, had always supported their own poor; but a big shift happened when bishops, now powerful local leaders, became patrons of the poor and on the basis of the scriptures urged their congregations to give for general poor relief. That this went beyond cultural norms is substantiated by the fact that in the early 360s Julian, the apostate Emperor, tried to get his restored pagan institutions to emulate this.

In 368 famine struck central Turkey – the 'most severe one ever recorded'.[34] As ever, people hoarded grain, scarcity grew, prices soared. Basil, then assistant to the bishop of Caesarea, spent his own inheritance and got others to open up their stores, establishing soup kitchens for the starving masses. He preached a sermon which drew on Amos to call people to repentance – the unnatural winter drought and spring heat-wave were the result of sin. Now God had granted the rich an opportunity to discover that wealth is worth nothing in the face of death, and they should give, not stock-pile. He sketched stories of Elijah and Moses; he alluded to the parable of the sheep and the goats. He called on the congregation to emulate the earliest Christians in Jerusalem who had all things in common, and follow the many examples of brotherly love in Old and New Testaments. Later, himself now Bishop, Basil founded the Basilcias on his nearby estate – a 'new city' his friend called it.[35] Here, there were quarters for the bishop and his guests, a hostel for travellers, a monastery, and a hospice for the poor and for the sick, including lepers. His friend and younger brother, both called Gregory, preached sermons in support of this project, insisting that love of humanity is what makes us most like God, and most like Jesus who became human for our sake. Love is the first and greatest of the commandments, and love of the poor is its most excellent form. Even lepers, whose illness led to poverty, disfigurement and ostracism from society, are made in God's image. Christ's example, in bearing our weaknesses and suffering pain for us, should transform our attitudes. We become divine, fellow-heirs with Christ, through imitating God, who sends rain on just and unjust alike.

Soon the reciprocity of rich and poor would become a standard idea, the poor offering prayer for the salvation of the rich in return for the sustenance received.[36] From our perspective preaching like this never effected genuine social change – indeed it encouraged the kind of top-down patronizing charity from a position of power which traps the poor in their poverty, but still it was as much a social revolution as any other consequence of Constantine's conversion. The Gregories show how the whole concept of Christian charity was challenging the accepted practice of municipal good works. It was no longer right to restrict benevolence to those who belonged, or to shun those feared because of contagion. The grounds for universal appeal on behalf of those afflicted lay in the fact of Christ's identification with the poor.

God's mission and Christendom

The Church had always believed that

- it was God's mission to establish divine rule over the earth by victory over the powers of evil, and
- God's purpose is that through the Church all should come to recognize and worship the one and only God, the Creator,
  - under whose providence and oversight all history was played out, as the fulfilment of prophecy demonstrated,
  - whose will was to be obeyed, everyone being accountable for the way they lived their lives, and whose writ ran even in the secret places of the heart, but
  - whose grace and love of humanity was shown in the incarnation, death and resurrection of Jesus Christ,
  - through whom mercy and forgiveness, life and salvation were granted to all who believe, receive the medicine of immortality in the Eucharist and live a pure and holy life.

What Constantine seemed to promise was the possibility of all this being fulfilled on earth, of uniting the whole world in peace and recognition of the truth about the one God, ensuring proper worship of that one God, the end of idolatry and heresy, and a re-education of the masses, changing people's behaviour to accord with the dominical command to love God and neighbour, through preaching, example and legislation.

But the outcome was problematic. In spite of Christianity's emphasis on love, even of one's enemy, coercion became justified as a kind of love, forcing schismatics, heretics, Jews and pagans to conform for their own good – Augustine, for example, called in imperial troops against the Donatists, the dominant, puritanical 'denomination' in North Africa. Violence, even on the part of monks studying to reach 'passionlessness' and become like God, became acceptable in the war against untruth, and the temptations of power and wealth corrupted Church leaders – in struggles over doctrine, evidence of ethical misbehaviour played a very large role! So earthly power proved the best way to undermine some of the key characteristics of Jesus' teaching, and those who tried to maintain monastic purity and prophetic witness in a bishop's palace found their throne too hot for a hair-shirt – John Chrysostom lost out when he dared to call the empress Jezebel! And then there is the issue of religious superstition – people still expected to get benefits from divine powers in return for vows and offerings. As the civic religion of the imperial court and the popular religion of the people, Christianity had to become what people wanted, a reliable source of relief from the problems of life, its ill-health and bad luck, an almost magical solution which put you in touch with supernatural power. As a student I had a professor who liked to contrast Christianity with religion. It would be possible to argue that the Church did not look much like a religion before Constantine, but took on the trappings of ancient paganism when it was adopted as the Empire's uniting religion.

In the early 1980s a book was published entitled *Constantine versus Christ*:[37] basically the argument was that the essential thrust of Christianity was corrupted by Constantine, who was never really converted to Christianity. But surely it all depends on your perception of what the gospel of Jesus Christ is. Is it after all God's mission to transform society and unite everyone in a common faith? We should by now be aware what that might mean: convert everyone, suppress all alternatives, and limit freedom of religion. What else does the experience of Christendom tell us, along with the centuries of conflicts in which religion has notoriously been not merely complicit but a crucial factor? 'We often think of difference as something that needs to be overcome to reach unity, which usually leads to laminating people so that everyone fits into the box', wrote someone recently.[38] That is a kind of unity that implies, if not coercion, then compromise – wishy-washy tolerance papering over conflict. But suppose true unity involves complexity, and celebrating the amazing diversity of God's world, including differences within the human species and their cultures?

So I wonder whether we should be nostalgic for a time when religion was not privatized and Christianity had greater public influence; I wonder whether we should long for a more effective establishment of the Church, for a Christian majority, for the coming great united Church of the ecumenical movement. Surely we value freedom of religion, personal choice and commitment, democracy and pluralism. But if that is so, what does it mean for God's kingdom on earth? What is appropriate Christian mission in a post-Christian society? Should we perhaps be more like the pre-Constantinian Church, the hidden soul within the body politic?

Notes

1. For the political situation, see Timothy Barnes, *Constantine and Eusebius*, Cambridge, MA: Harvard University Press, 1981. There is no attempt to document everything in this chapter, much of which is standard history. Some contentious or specific points, however, are referenced, together with suggestions for further reading.
2. Ramsay MacMullen, *Christianizing the Roman Empire: AD 100–400*, New Haven and London: Yale University Press, 1984, Chapter V.
3. For comments on Christian art here and below, see Robin M. Jensen, 'Towards a Christian Material Culture' in Margaret M. Mitchell and Frances M. Young (eds), *The Cambridge History of Christianity: Origins to Constantine*, Cambridge: Cambridge University Press, 2006, pp. 568–85.
4. See Alistair Kee, *Constantine versus Christ: The Triumph of Ideology*, London: SCM Press, 1982; he argues the case against this being a Christian symbol, and robustly challenges the notion that Constantine's religion was Christianity.
5. Barnes (1981) upholds, against other scholars, the view that Eusebius is correct in saying Constantine tried to outlaw sacrifice; in general he presents Constantine as a Christian with specifically Christian policies.
6. See Barnes (1981), especially Chapter IV.
7. MacMullen (1984), pp. 49–50. Chapter VI notes the nonreligious reasons for conversion, including financial issues, grain doles, fear of the emperor, career advantage, etc. Barnes (1981), p. 247, argues that there was a deliberate attempt to suppress paganism.
8. See Raymond Van Dam, *Becoming Christian: The Conversion of Roman Cappadocia*, Philadelphia: Pennsylvania University Press, 2003.
9. Such accusations were used against those deemed to be heretics: for example Cyril of Jerusalem, Athanasius, *et al*. The charges against John Chrysostom involved the mishandling of cases of corruption among bishops. For fuller details, see Frances Young with Andrew Teal, *From Nicaea to Chalcedon*, second edition, London: SCM Press, 2010.
10. For fuller details of Synesius' career, see Young with Teal (2010).
11. See Mark Edwards, 'The Constantinian Circle and the *Oration to the Saints*' in Mark Edwards, Martin Goodman and Simon Price (eds), *Apologetics in the Roman Empire: Pagans, Jews and Christians*, Oxford: Oxford University Press, 1999, pp. 251–75, to which I am indebted for many of the points made here and below.
12. Edwards (1999), p. 257.

13. *Oration to the Saints* 23; ET E. C. Richardson, *Nicene and Post-Nicene Fathers* II, vol. I, p. 579, altered.

14. MacMullen (1984), especially Chapters V, VI and X.

15. For the complex issues raised by Eusebius' work on Constantine, see Averil Cameron, 'Eusebius' *Vita Constantini* and the Construction of Constantine' in M. J. Edwards and Simon Swain (eds), *Portraits. Biographical Representation in the Greek and Latin Literature of the Roman Empire*, Oxford: Clarendon, 1997, pp. 145–74. Cf. H. A. Drake, *In Praise of Constantine*, Berkeley: University of California Press, 1976; and Barnes (1981).

16. *Life of Constantine* 10; ET E. C. Richardson, *Nicene and Post-Nicene Fathers* II, vol. I, p. 484.

17. In many ways the old 'Ruler-cult' is presupposed, but Christianized. Constantine still stands in the same kind of 'intermediate position' between gods and humans; 'standing at the apex of the hierarchy of the Roman Empire', the ruler was represented as a 'universal god' who 'offered the hope of order and stability', but he also needed 'divine protection'. See S. R. F. Price, *Rituals and Power: The Roman Imperial Cult in Asia Minor*, Cambridge: Cambridge University Press, 1984.

18. On Socrates, see Theresa Urbainczyk, *Socrates of Constantinople: Historian of Church and State*, Ann Arbor: University of Michigan Press, 1997. The quotation in this paragraph is from the preface to Socrates' *Church History* V; ET A. T. Zenos in *Nicene and Post-Nicene Fathers* II, vol. 2, p. 118.

19. For recently revised perspectives on the so-called Arian controversy, see for example Lewis Ayres, *Nicaea and its Legacy: An Approach to Fourth-Century Trinitarian Theology*, Oxford: Oxford University Press, 2004.

20. Sozomen, *Church History* IX. 9.

21. See Young with Teal (2010) for more details concerning John Chrysostom.

22. Socrates, *Church History* V. 16.

23. Sozomen, *Church History* VII. 15.

24. Socrates, *Church History* V. 17.

25. Elizabeth S. Bolman, 'The Enigmatic Coptic Galaktrophousa and the Cult of the Virgin Mary in Egypt' in Maria Vassilaki (ed.), *Images of the Mother of God: Perceptions of the Theotokos in Byzantium*, Aldershot: Ashgate, 2005.

26. *Church History* VII. 18.

27. In a letter preserved in Latin translation among the correspondence of Jerome.

28. See Frances M. Young, Prelude to *The Cambridge History of Christianity*, pp. 1–34.

29. Theodoret, *The Cure of Pagan Maladies*.

30. Stephen Benko, *The Virgin Goddess: Studies in the Pagan and Christian Roots of Mariology*, Studies in the History of Religions LIX, Leiden: Brill, 1993.

31. Epiphanius, *Panarion* 79.
32. For a fuller introduction to the monastic movement, and bibliography, see Young with Teal (2010), Chapter 3.
33. For fuller treatment of these texts and their implications, see Susan Holman, *The Hungry are Dying*, Oxford: Oxford University Press, 2001.
34. Gregory Nazianzen, *Oration* 43.34; ET C. G. Browne and J. E. Swallow in *Nicene and Post-Nicene Fathers* II, vol. 7, p. 407.
35. Gregory Nazianzen, *Oration* 43.63.
36. Especially in the preaching of John Chrysostom; see further Young with Teal (2010).
37. Kee (1982).
38. Christian Salenson, unpublished papers for the L'Arche community in France.

5

Reflections for Today's Church

MORNA HOOKER AND

FRANCES YOUNG

What mission? (Morna Hooker)

Our theme in this book has been 'mission', something that has been an essential part of the Christian gospel from the beginning. Indeed, since the word 'gospel' translates a Greek work meaning 'good news', it is clear that Christians are expected to pass it on. Not surprisingly, mission has always been part of Methodist belief and practice also. The Arminian view of salvation adopted by John Wesley led to the conviction that 'all can be saved', and so compelled him to evangelize. Mission was a theme emphasized by the President of the Methodist Conference, when he and the Vice-President addressed the Synod of the Church of England in February 2010. Shortly afterwards, they (together with the General Secretary) sent a Pastoral Letter to the Methodist people. I was struck, when reading this, by the number of times they used the word 'mission'. It seemed to occur in every paragraph! We are agreed, then, that Christians have been commissioned – commission-ed – to spread the gospel. They have been entrusted to pass it on. But how are they to do that?

Two models

There are two very different ways of answering that question, and they produce two very different models of mission. On the one hand, there are those who think of mission primarily in terms of *preaching* the gospel, together with giving personal testimony. The model of a big evangelical rally immediately comes to mind. Some of us are old enough to remember the vast audiences addressed by

Billy Graham at Wembley Stadium. The aim of such evangelistic rallies was to 'save souls'. The preaching and the follow-up counselling concentrated on each individual's relationship with God.

On the other hand, there are those who have seen mission primarily in terms of helping those in need. The roots of this approach are found in the conviction that Christians are summoned to share in Christ's own mission by bringing healing and hope to the sick and hungry, poor and imprisoned. The model that comes to mind here is that of the various city missions throughout the land, many of them run by the Salvation Army or by the Methodist Church. The West London Mission itself is an example of how the gospel has been interpreted in terms of practical social action. Christians have seen their mission as a summons to transform the world, and have even spoken optimistically of building the kingdom of God on earth.

Here, then, are two very different models of mission. The strength of the first is that it never loses sight of the importance of the gospel for each individual believer. But that stress on the individual explains the inherent danger. It is all too easy to be so overwhelmed by joy in a personal experience of God that religion becomes self-centred – a matter of me and God, with the rest of the world ignored. When that happens, the Christian community can become a holy huddle, isolated from the world outside. That ties up with the attitude I looked at in the first chapter, which saw holiness in terms of a separation from everything that might contaminate one. The strength of the second model is that it embraces the world, and remembers the biblical insistence that love of God goes hand in hand with love of one's neighbour. The danger this time is that it is God who is sometimes pushed to the periphery and is forgotten. Mission is no longer doing *the gospel*, if we forget that it is rooted in the good news about God.

So are we to preach the gospel or to do it? As with many questions, this one is in fact inappropriate, since we will surely want to say 'both'. And indeed, our big city missions combine preaching and practice. We need only think of Donald Soper, preaching at Kingsway Hall, arguing on his soap box in Hyde Park and running the West London Mission, to see how the two belong together.

As to *why* they belong together, well for this there is a good biblical basis. Once again I appeal to the Greek – this time to the Greek word *logos*. As we saw in Chapter 1, *logos*, or 'word', refers not just to what is spoken but to what is done. In the beginning, God spoke – and it was so.[1] God's words, said the prophet, do not return to him empty.[2] In John, we read that the word became flesh – and that he spoke and did the words and works of God. Word and action belong together.

Holiness

In the first chapter, I stressed that the biblical understanding of holiness was rooted in the command to be holy as God is holy. Holiness concerned not only personal piety but acting as God would act – the God who is righteous, and whose justice is tempered with mercy. It is not surprising that the first Christians, believing themselves to be God's holy people, understood their mission in terms of spreading the good news and of doing it. These two aspects have belonged together in Christian mission from the beginning. We have seen already how early Christians were concerned to care for those in need. And since this book is in part a celebration of 250 years of Methodism in the West End, it seems appropriate to remember how, at Oxford, Charles Wesley founded the 'Holy Club' – a group that was later joined by John, on his return to Oxford in 1729. Members of the Holy Club strove on the one hand for personal piety, rooted in Bible study, prayer and self-examination; on the other, they cared for the needy, taking food and clothes to the poor, and visiting those in prison or the workhouse. The Holy Club reflected the biblical understanding of what it meant to be a holy people: love for God and love for one's neighbours.

Following his so-called 'conversion', John Wesley explained his mission in the following terms: he and his brother had been sent 'to reform the nation, particularly the Church, and to spread scriptural holiness over the land'.[3] Scriptural holiness, he now realized, was nothing less than 'the image of God stamped on the heart . . . the whole mind which was in Christ Jesus'.[4] The ideas are certainly scriptural, and the language echoes that of Paul. Wesley continued to emphasize holiness as love for God and love for one's neighbour. No wonder he believed that his mission was 'to reform the nation'.

'To reform the nation, particularly the Church.' The Church Wesley had in mind was, of course, the Church of England. His aim was to reform the nation by recalling the Church to its mission. In that he failed, and was obliged to turn to other means, appointing preachers to take the gospel to those outside the Church, establishing Methodist societies and class meetings to care for those within. Leaders of class meetings were expected to see their members at least once a week, 'in order to enquire how their souls prosper', and 'to receive what they are willing to give toward the relief of the poor'.[5] 'Holiness' meant not only personal piety, but concern for one's neighbour's welfare.

Mission today

So what of mission in the twenty-first century? What should *we* be doing? One thing is plain: we should not expect the answer to be the same for all. Paul's analogy of the body springs to mind. The Spirit pours out a great variety of gifts on his Church. Some may be called to preach the gospel – but not all. Some will be called to teach. But many more will be called to *do* the gospel. Although some Christians – notably some of our political leaders – insist that their beliefs are a private matter, and apparently irrelevant to the world in which they live, there has been a growing conviction in recent years that Christian faith must be expressed in social holiness and justice.[6] That could mean going out, getting involved in politics and campaigns, offering help, visiting, befriending the lonely and unhappy; or it could mean inviting people in, forming small groups where people will feel at home. And many others will play their part by supporting and praying for the work done by others. In 1 Corinthians, Paul lists the various gifts of the Spirit, insisting that the greatest gifts are not those that bring glory to an individual, but those that build up the community. That is why the greatest gift of all, as we learn in 1 Corinthians 13, is love.

In another famous passage, Paul describes how he has gone about the task of mission. He has, he tells us, 'become all things to all people'. In order to win those under the law, he behaved as though he himself were still under the law, and to those outside the law, he behaved as one outside the law, while to the weak he himself became weak.[7] Paul's understanding of his mission is clearly modelled on the example of Christ, who was born under the law in order to redeem those under the law, who became sin in order that the sinful might be made righteous, and who became poor in order to make the poor rich.[8] Here is the pattern for all mission: empathy – getting alongside those in need – in order to share with them the blessings of the gospel. What Christ himself did is the model for all who are members of his body.

* * *

Ways of mission (Frances Young)

Two models of mission have been introduced, the evangelistic and the practical. Reflecting on the earlier chapters, I suspect we could chart across them four or five different approaches or methods: (1) evangelical preaching; (2) the creation of networks – groups to which people belong and where they learn to love one another; then (3) reaching out in practical ways to show love of neighbour; (4) engaging in politics so as to transform society; and (5) ecumenical activity, on the grounds that Church unity is a pre-requisite for mission – how can you preach a gospel of reconciliation if churches are not reconciled with one another? Let us consider this range of approaches.

Evangelical preaching

Since the eighteenth-century Evangelical Revival, mission has been primarily associated with preaching the 'simple' gospel, in the highways and byways, in camp meetings, in town centres and on street corners, in football stadiums and so on. John Wesley provides an exemplar: though reluctant, he was persuaded by George Whitefield into 'field preaching'. To quote his *Journal* for Monday, 2 March 1739,

At 4.00 in the afternoon I submitted to be more vile, and proclaimed in the highways the glad tidings of salvation, speaking from a little eminence in a ground adjoining the city to about 3,000 people.

Once begun, it continued. 'I look upon all the world as my parish,' he affirmed, when other clergy complained of his trespassing on their patch. Wesley rode the length and breadth of the country, facing mobs, heckling, insults and missiles for the sake of preaching the gospel. His *Journal* speaks of crowds numbering sometimes 20,000, sometimes 30,000, and usually describes their response as listening in silence with rapt attention, though there are some accounts of strange happenings which anticipate phenomena found in the twentieth-century charismatic movement. This approach remains influential; but if the picture of the early Church in Chapter 3 is right, it is an approach that has been read back to the early period rather than representing the way things were back then. Preaching proved not to be the important factor in Christianity's spread.

There are some other striking differences between the early Church and evangelical missions since the eighteenth century. In a nominally Christian society, Wesley could presume what the early Christians were seeking to establish – one God, Creator of all, who makes ethical demands. His gospel concerned God's mercy, love and forgiveness. The outcome expected was exemplified in Wesley's own so-called conversion experience on 24 May 1739: at a meeting in Aldersgate Street, someone was reading from Luther's Preface to the Epistle to the Romans, and 'about a quarter before nine, while he was describing the change which God works in the heart through faith in Christ', Wesley says:

> I felt my heart strangely warmed. I felt I did trust in Christ, Christ alone for salvation; and an assurance was given me that he had taken away *my* sins, even *mine*, and saved *me* from the law of sin and death.

Thus the so-called 'simple gospel' came to be widely understood as focusing on the cross as a sacrifice offered on behalf of each individual sinner, who is invited to know Jesus as his or her personal Saviour and friend. Because this gospel has been preached in nominally Christian societies, it has been taken to be only authentic if each person makes it their own. I suspect that this tradition has contributed not a little to the individualism of our culture,[9] though doubtless consumerism and choice have reinforced the idea that religion is a matter of private commitment rather than publicly acknowledged truth. A claim to Truth (with a capital 'T') is now particularly hard to make in our post-Christian, relativistic society – but Truth was what was at stake in the early centuries. Conversion to Christianity meant a shift from one world-view to another.

Networks and practical outreach

Conversion in the early centuries also meant changing from one life-style to another. Now that is certainly a common feature – in the eighteenth century, as in the early Church, converts were meant to aim for holiness and 'doing the gospel', the second model already explored. But this was aided by belonging to like-minded communities, or networks. In his *Journal* for 25 August 1763 Wesley wrote:

> I was more convinced than ever that the preaching like an apostle without joining together those that are awakened and training them up in the ways of God, is only begetting children for the murderer [= devil]. How much preaching has there been for these 20 years all over Pembrokeshire! But no regular societies, no discipline, no order or correction; and the consequence is that nine in ten of the once-awakened are now faster asleep than ever.

So Wesley's class meetings confirm the kind of account of the early Church given earlier. Fundamental to the spread of Christianity was drawing people into groups and networks and giving them a sense of belonging. Generally speaking, this approach has not been so clearly articulated as an approach to mission, but historians suggest it was what made Wesley successful. Our exploration of the early spread of Christianity suggests the same thing, and it is probably now a significant element in the spread of the Alpha Course. It is an important approach, not least because it is also fundamental to effecting the changes in people's lives that reflect God's holiness. You need confidence in God's love, and the love of your brothers and sisters in Christ, in order to have the love that can break across boundaries and learn to love the stranger and the enemy as well as the neighbour.

Changing society

Some say that by changing society you push forward God's mission, which is to bring in the kingdom of God. This has inspired politicians in the past and to some extent still does in our society. It is the kind of thing that Constantine and his successors down the ages tried to do by establishing Christianity as the state religion, and there is some warrant for it in the Bible.

But was Europe ever really Christian?[10] John Wesley would certainly have replied that eighteenth-century Britain was not, despite the acknowledged establishment of religion in society. Recent history tells us that attempts to impose fairness become totalitarian (as in communism), welfare systems are all too often exploited by the selfish, and in any case force has always been needed to impose law and order. Christian theology, with its emphasis on the corporate nature of human sin and human failure to live up to what God intended, can offer good reasons why it is hard to create a society where equals respect one another, where poverty is ended, where conflict and war are overcome, and those who need care and support are lovingly looked after. It seems that change in society can only come if people are changed, but then often people are trapped by society and constrained by circumstances – so you need both! But we all know that power corrupts – to the dismay of many Christian believers, avowedly Christian leaders like Bush and Blair ended up engaging in war, and identifying their mission with God's mission like Constantine.

Nevertheless, it is hardly surprising that Christian values inspire people to try and change the world, and there are examples where this has genuinely made a difference – the abolition of slavery provides a classic case. Prophetic critique and political action must surely constitute significant approaches to mission. But such activity needs to be self-critical. To take action 'bottom-up' rather than 'top-down' may be a better approach in our democratic, post-Christendom society. Being the leaven in the lump, or the soul in the body (as that early Christian apologist put it) might be a better way than seeking direct political influence.

Ecumenism

So we come to the case for ecumenism as essential to mission. But Constantine's struggle for Church unity might pose a few *caveats* here too. I speak as a life-long ecumenist, and as a theologian who has learnt much from other Christian traditions; but I now find myself asking, 'What kind of unity?' The search for unity so often seems to generate yet more splinter groups, to require looking for the lowest common denominator, or to involve giving more power to the powerful – not least because it is envisaged in terms of one great unified and uniform institution. I shall never forget listening to Spanish Protestants at the World Faith and Order conference in Santiago de Compostela in 1993 as they talked about not being allowed to exist under Franco. It made me think again about the importance of religious freedom. Surely, the model of reconciliation was better represented by the Franciscans allowing the small group of Spanish Protestants to borrow their large basilica so that they could break bread with their Protestant brothers and sisters from around the globe. We need, not a unified top-down totalitarian ecclesiastical institution, surely, but public demonstrations that, though diverse, we Christians love one another. I seriously wonder now whether ecumenism really needs a different model of unity.

So how do we embody God's mission? I would not claim to be an expert here, but surely we can learn something from the earlier chapters. As already suggested, we could start by acknowledging that there are many different ways of being holy and many different callings, but there are perhaps some more specific things we should draw out of our studies and reflections:

- We should accept that mission is about more than individual conversion, yet it is vital for persons to discover the love of God deep in their hearts, if they are to produce living that is loving – and sometimes evangelical preaching can be a catalyst for changed lives which reflect God's holiness.
- We should note the importance of incorporating ourselves and others in loving networks where God's love is received as well as offered, and which are open to draw in strangers and seekers, the lonely and the lost.
- We should commit ourselves, our groups, our churches to take action, appropriate to circumstances, to express God's love for others. Examples are aplenty. In our democratic society, it might still mean for some entering politics at local or national level to try and effect change; but particularly taking our cues from what we found the early Church doing, we might suggest: (1) welcoming migrants of all kinds, asylum

seekers, people lost and lonely in big cities and strange cultures; (2) finding ways to support people who are elderly, sick, disabled, families in crisis; (3) working with other networks to challenge poverty and specific injustices, war and the trade in armaments, the trafficking of women and children; (4) simply going about our business with integrity and respect for those we work with; (5) engaging in intercessory prayer, giving the widow's mite to charity – even the housebound can embody God's mission in such ways.

* * *

The challenge (Morna Hooker)

Matthew's Gospel ends with the Risen Jesus commanding his disciples to go to all the nations, and make them his disciples. They are to baptize them and teach them what he has taught them. Disciples – a word that means 'learners' – must be taught. This emphasis on teaching may surprise us – but it shouldn't. What, after all, did 'the nations' know about Israel's God? The early missionaries often had to start from scratch. If they appealed to the scriptures, then it was necessary for their converts to discover what those scriptures said. I often wonder what Paul's converts made of his somewhat convoluted arguments! As a Jew who was trained in biblical exegesis, he naturally began from scripture and used the exegetical methods of the day. He did his best to explain to his converts the riches of the Christian gospel, but I suspect that he often left them floundering – which would explain, of course, why there were so many misunderstandings of the gospel, and why he had to write to the churches he had founded, spelling out its implications.

The Church's teaching mission

It is hardly surprising then if, as we were reminded earlier, Christianity seemed, in its early years, more like a school than a religion.[11] If one were to be a Christian, it was necessary to give an account of the faith which was in one. In later centuries, however, with the rise of creeds, faith came to be understood as '*the* faith', agreement to a set of beliefs rather than trust in the living God. To its shame, the Church came to insist on adherence to set dogmas, and persecuted those who refused to subscribe to them. At the Reformation, Catholics and Protestants burnt one another at the stake for holding different teachings. Sadly, that was not the only period in Church history when Christian love was replaced by intolerance.

In the twenty-first century, we are appalled. Christianity, we insist, is a living faith, not an agreement to dogma! True – but perhaps we have swung too far the other way, and neglected the need for teaching in our churches. Sermons, we insist, are not the place for teaching. True again – but where is sound teaching to be given? All too often, preachers shy away from using what they have been taught about the Bible, for fear of upsetting the faithful. If faith is so easily destroyed, then we must wonder whether it is really firmly based! Preachers should certainly draw on the work of scholars, and they are denying their congregations the riches of the gospel – what Paul termed 'the meat' as distinct from the 'milk'[12] – if they fail to do so. Congregations deserve honesty in preaching.

Sadly, many young people today lack knowledge of the Bible and the Christian faith. Our Sunday Schools are almost extinct. Schools teach little about the content of the Christian faith, since that could be seen as indoctrination, and neglect to teach basic knowledge of the Bible, depriving children of the key to understanding centuries of music, literature and art. Methodism's class meetings rarely meet today – though there are some exceptions, and a few churches even organize lecture-series such as the Hugh Price Hughes lectures! But by and large the Church neglects its teaching mission. Even the great hymns of Charles Wesley – all of them statements of theology, designed to convey the fundamentals of the faith – are being pushed out in favour of modern songs with little theological content. How are our people to know what the Christian gospel is about?

There are, of course, examples of successful teaching missions. Mention has been made of the Alpha Course. It is not just the meals that make them attractive! The fact that they are based on small groups, where a few people get to know one another well, is clearly a key factor, but the numbers attracted to these courses suggests that there is a hunger for teaching. Alpha's aim is, of course, to make converts, but they have combined the evangelistic appeal with teaching. Methodism's 'Disciple' course aims at teaching those in the Church, rather than bringing in those outside. The adult Sunday Schools in America have a similar aim. Disciples – learners – have to be taught, and the Church that neglects to build up its own members in the faith is not ready to engage in mission to the world. Jesus, we are told, called his disciples to be with him, and to go out. Being with him came first, and for almost his entire ministry they were with him and he taught them. Only then were they ready to be sent out.

Reforming the nation

And after sitting at the feet of Jesus, we are sent out to challenge the world – sent, in John Wesley's phrase, 'to reform the nation'. The nation is in no less need of reform than it was in his day. We are confronted by injustice, immorality, poverty, and a social divide, which has been described as splitting London into two cities. I referred on an earlier occasion to the *Evening Standard*'s report on poverty.[13] In one of its leaders, the paper describes the deprivation uncovered by its reporters as 'an affront to a civilized city'.[14] We must surely add: an 'affront also to God'. There is plenty for us to challenge in the city today.

But if we are to tackle the problems, we need to understand their causes. What has led to this devastating picture? The modern emphasis on the individual is surely part of the problem. Individual excellence is praised, but competition means that there are losers as well as winners. Status is prized – in society, in schools, even in the Church. And it's not all down to Constantine! Read the early chapters of 1 Corinthians and you will see that little has changed over the years. Greed makes individuals demand huge salaries, making the divide between rich and poor ever greater. The love of status and riches and power brings corruption and sleaze.

How are we to challenge these things? How are we to cope with them when they impinge on our own lives? How do we function in the workplace? How do we exist in a competitive society? And how do we do the best for our children without becoming a part of the competitive culture?

The biblical advice is clear. Paul writes, 'Do not be conformed to this world, but be transformed by the renewing of your minds'

(Romans 12.2). In other words, have the mind of Christ. But how are we to demonstrate the mind of Christ in the situations in which we find ourselves?

* * *

The Church as a learning community (Frances Young)

We have seen how the early Church in Graeco-Roman society looked more like a school than a religion. Christianity, like Judaism and Islam, has always been a 'book' religion, with a strong ethical stance; it also changed the perception of religion itself by making belief so central. So how much do we need to *know*? Do we all have to be theologians?

Well, the 'school' to which the early Christians belonged was not elitist or exclusive. My son, Arthur, now in his forties, not only uses a wheelchair and has no self-help skills, but also has no language and his understanding is probably about the level of a 15-month-old; he was baptized as an infant, therefore belongs to Christ, participates somewhat unconventionally in worship, and at times ministers to me and also to others. The point surely is that anyone can be embraced by God's grace whether they know it or not. But the Church – the community of Christians – needs to have a collective understanding of what it is all about, and confessing Christians with intelligence and education need to love God with their minds as well as their heart, soul and strength, so as to give an account of the faith that is in them.

Mission is tough in European society because religion is widely despised. The common sense of our culture is anti-religious and the dominant intellectual understanding is that Christianity is outmoded. You know the kind of thing:

- Religion is positively dangerous, the cause of violence and intolerance, while Christianity is kill-joy, repressing everything worthwhile in human life, such as the enjoyment of sex, alcohol and good food.
- Religion turns people into extremists, and Christianity turns them into hypocrites – volunteers at a church-based day centre for old people are thought to be buying their ticket to heaven.

- Religion discriminates against women and gays, and where Christianity upholds its traditionally strict sexual codes it encourages clandestine abuse.
- Christianity affirms its traditional stance against abortion in the face of excessive population growth, and against euthanasia where compassion often demands it.
- Religion is unnecessary to explain life, the universe or anything, and most people are not religious anyhow.
- Religious experience counts for nothing – it's all in the mind! – while conversion-experiences happen to the unbalanced and immature.

British society does not directly persecute and generally avoids creating martyrs, but Christianity bears the brunt of satire, caricature and ridicule in our post-Christian society, in TV comedy, cartoons and books like *The God Delusion*.[15] Some of it is deserved.

Like Christians in the Roman Empire, so now in our post-Christian society, religious people are marginalized; they are treated as an anomaly in a society which is secular, apart from some surviving bits of 'civic religion' for the sake of history and tradition. There is anxiety about religious 'enthusiasm', as there was in John Wesley's day, and serious belief is not taken seriously. The reasons may be different, but to own one's faith in public means sticking out like a sore thumb, as it did, with potentially more dangerous consequences, for the early Christians. As Prime Minister, Blair 'did not do religion'. Britain has been called the hardest mission field in the world.

To meet this situation we need to know what we are talking about; we need to be open to responsive change; we need to be seen to be challenging injustice and lack of compassion. But we are deeply divided about key issues, traditionalists resisting change, appealing to scripture, or tradition, or both. Many of those contentious issues have their roots in the way the early Church conformed to, or challenged, Graeco-Roman culture. Conformity meant patriarchy and a failure to challenge the institutional subordination of women, or indeed slavery; but the problems with respect to sexuality arise from Christian challenges to the prevailing culture, and the strict sexual ethic we noted in earlier chapters. That is true, too, of the ethical issues around taking life. Theirs was a society where abortion, infanticide and suicide were socially acceptable – suicide being widely regarded among the elite as an honourable way out of, for example, a difficult political situation. Christian opposition to prevailing attitudes came from their teaching that life is God's good gift. This principle also led to the rejection of contraception. The question for us is whether the theological argument leads to the same conclusions about ethics in a world which is over-populated and where medical science officiously keeps people alive in situations where nature, left to itself, would terminate. Does such a changed situation suggest, not that the theological principle should be compromised, but that it might be interpreted differently, and even challenge some other endemic attitudes in society? After all, much of the pressure for abortion and euthanasia comes from the assumption that this life should be perfect. I am not sure that the elimination of all who are profoundly disabled would be a good thing for society. It is often in their company that one finds the deepest experiences of the gift of the Spirit – love, joy, peace, patience, kindness, generosity, faithfulness, gentleness and self-control (Galatians 5.22–23). And paradoxically it is the same attitudes which foster an unwillingness in our society to accept death as part of life. Perhaps the most important thing we might learn from early Christians is something of their confidence in the face of death – for just as life is God's good gift, so also is new life through Christ's resurrection.

Like the early Church, we need to challenge the culture in which we find ourselves, and this might mean challenge with respect to such basic issues as life and death, the materialist economic principles that have become the prime measure of social good, the success-values which marginalize those unable to compete, and so on. To do this we need, collectively, a deeper awareness of our own identity (or identities) as Christians, a more subtle understanding of our sacred texts, with their liability to provide warrant for such things as slavery and patriarchy – not to mention their inner contradictions – and a greater awareness of our history (or histories) as churches. All of that would mean becoming more 'school'-like.

But does that imply going back to being dogmatic about the truth? I am not sure that it does. I think it does mean having a sense of Christian identity, a kind of ecumenical vision of Christianity – over time as well as across denominations – and from that identifying a few key principles that provide the warrant for a holy lifestyle in this new cultural context. Such key principles might include:

- the affirmation that this is God's world, not ours, a point which should produce (1) an environmental awareness which challenges our anthropocentrism (the assumption that everything was created for the sake of humankind, and so we can do what we like with the natural world), and (2) a universal rather than exclusive view of humanity – since all belong to the one Creator God;
- the confession that Jesus embodies a way to be followed, because he was and is all of God that could be expressed in human form, and also what human beings were meant to be as God's image;
- commitment to the way, or Spirit, of Jesus as the way of love, involving love of God, love of neighbour (which, if we take the Good Samaritan seriously, includes the stranger, the foreigner, the person different or 'other' – in other words, not like us), and even love of enemy.

As a theologian I would want to spell all that out in much fuller Trinitarian terms, and show how it coheres with the identity bequeathed to us by our history. But in our society we are not going to get very far by preaching dogmatic truths, or dragooning people into the kingdom of God – we are by now all too aware that power corrupts, and that Christendom lost Christ in crusades and heresy-hunts.

If we start with these principles, then the reality of God's kingdom as fundamentally different from the kingdoms of this world becomes clear. In a funny kind of way, God chooses to be the hidden King, who does not coerce but invites, and woos us through Christ into living as if God's values were realizable, despite our failure and sin.

Surely mission is fundamentally about responding to God's call to have the mind that was in Christ Jesus and express it in daily life in relation to the 150 contacts which, it is said, each of us can cope with. But we need to know why we do it. Christianity did not spread in the Roman world through public preaching – the content was not what first attracted. However, it did have content – an understanding of the way things are – a philosophy, if you like, which undergirded the Christian way of life, and which those who joined would learn.

* * *

Pluralism and the gospel (Frances Young)

One of the main themes of the historical chapters has been the early Church's opposition to idolatry; faced with a thoroughly religious culture, Christians were conscientious objectors to the false worship all around them. Surely we have to abandon traditional approaches to idolatry if we are going to live tolerantly in a pluralist society.

It is worth remembering that idolatry for the early Church was the powerful religious apparatus of the entire culture. Nineteenth-century missionaries treated Hinduism in India as idolatry, and there are considerable analogies with religion in the Roman empire, in terms of social position, the variety of gods, the mythology, the images – even a unifying philosophy. But some of the critique of idolatry was born, in the early Church, of deliberate distortion, and in the nineteenth century, of misunderstanding; furthermore, there is nothing similar in cultures shaped by Islam or Christianity. Nevertheless, there might be good reasons for de-mythologizing idolatry in terms of what people are most devoted to – in the West it has sometimes been identified as money, fashion, the latest must-have or pop-idol in our personality culture. Suppose, however, we define idols as man-made gods, then the atheists in our society are probably right to accuse all religious people of believing in idols – we all easily project onto the heavens the god we want. Let me quote from an early Greek philosopher words preserved by an early Christian:

> Ethiopians make their gods black with turned-up noses. Thracians make them with red hair and blue eyes; mortals think that gods are born and have their own food, voice and shape; but if oxen or lions had hands and could draw or produce images like men, horses would draw the shapes of the gods like horses, oxen like oxen, and [so on].

We need to hear for ourselves the critique of idolatry, not project it onto other religions.

In fact, the early Christians did not reject the insights of non-Christians into the truth. Justin Martyr in the second century thought that the Logos/Word of God was in Socrates, and

Constantine in the speech outlined in Chapter 4 suggested that, despite the wrong-headedness of the philosophers meddling with things beyond understanding, Plato did get an inkling of the truth. Jesus was the fulfilment of pagan as well as Jewish prophecies – sure, he trumped them all and was the full embodiment of the way, the truth and the life of God, but since God is the one true Creator of all, God is ultimately God for everyone whether they know it or not. We surely have something to learn from this perspective. The true God is bigger than any of our concepts or pictures of God. It is the experience of those engaged in dialogue with other faiths, that they learn things about their own in the process. Maybe we should adapt an old Middle Eastern parable which suggests that there is but one mountain, but we all find different routes up it, and see different, inevitably partial, views; if so, then the Christian spin on it might be that we believe that, as we make our ascent, God comes to meet us in Jesus Christ, but that need not rule out the views of other climbers up the mountain.

Now clearly the question about 'other faiths' applies not just to individuals but to whole communities, often defined not just by religion but by ethnicity. They sometimes say that Islamophobia is the new racism; that is because religion and ethnicity still run together to a fair extent, as they did in the Roman Empire. Religion is embedded in cultures – even post-Christian Britain has all kinds of Christian ideas often subconsciously built into its assumptions. Committed religious people have an identity shaped by their religious tradition, which is why religion rouses such passion, and why it gets sucked into conflicts – as, for example in Northern Ireland, the former Yugoslavia, and the Middle East. It is really important that in a world of identity-politics we respect the identity of others, while being properly self-conscious about our own identity. It does not help to find the lowest common denominator and say all religions are the same, though some people would like to believe that. However, it does help to work with those of other faiths – for peace, poverty relief, and so on, acknowledging that we have similar values and ethics; and dialogue which dissolves false preconceptions and enables learning from one another is also important for increasing mutual respect.

So what about mission? We should remember that it is God's mission, not ours, and not be too defensive or possessive about our role in that bigger picture. We should be confident about our identity as Christians and be prepared to give an account of the faith that is in us. But aggressive proselytism, I suggest, is not only counter-productive but untrue to the God of Christianity – the monarch who does not coerce, the King who empties himself and takes the way of the cross.

* * *

The message (Morna Hooker)

We live, we are told, in a post-Christian society. England – in spite of having an established Church – is no longer a Christian country. The churches which once dominated the London skyline are now dwarfed by buildings dedicated to the very different gods of business and finance. Equally significant, our churches stand side by side with mosques and temples. Other religions have come to stay.

Christians have always claimed that Christ is the fullest and clearest revelation of the one true God. Inevitably, other religions have been seen as inferior. In the nineteenth century, in the great period of mission expansion, Christians spoke disparagingly of the 'heathen' bowing down to idols of wood and stone. Missionary zeal demanded that they be converted. The choice was a clear one, between black and white, truth and falsehood, salvation and damnation.

Today, we are not so sure how to proceed. Certainly, we believe that God has revealed himself fully in the life, death and resurrection of Christ. But do Jews worship a *different* God? No, for it was the God who revealed himself to Israel who revealed himself through Christ. Do Muslims worship a different God? Or is it perhaps that their understanding of God is different? When we listen to the truths expressed in Sikh scriptures, do we wish to deny that God speaks through them? When Hindus worship many gods, are they perhaps pointing to different aspects of what God is? Even Buddhists, officially atheists, often seem to speak our language.

How, then, do we, who maintain that God spoke to us finally and fully through his Son, approach those of other faiths? Here are three tentative answers:

Biblical guidance

Let me take you back, once again, to the biblical scene. Centuries of tradition – and animosity – have conditioned us to think of Judaism and Christianity as different religions. But it was not always so. For much of the first century, Christianity was seen as a Jewish sect. Indeed, its relationship to Judaism was very similar to that of Methodism within the Church of England in the eighteenth century. In both cases, the tensions were such that the sect was eventually evicted. In the case of Judaism and Christianity, there was a fundamental issue of belief, and it centred on the person of Christ, but the earliest Christians were Jews, and they did not discard their belief in the God of Abraham, Isaac and Jacob when they acknowledged Jesus as Messiah. They continued to read the scriptures – the revelation of God to his people in the past. And when Paul embarked on his mission to the Gentiles, it was the 'true and living God' of the Old Testament that they embraced;[16] they learned about his will and about the salvation offered through Christ by listening to the Jewish scriptures. And though, in the second century, heretics – notably Marcion – denied that the God of Israel was the God who revealed himself in Christ, the Church continued to insist that they were the same.

Interestingly, the first Christians recognized truth in other religions also. Mention has been made of the later apologetic writers,[17] but already in the New Testament we find quotations from various philosophers,[18] and though these are in the nature of proverbs rather than theological statements, they suggest a recognition of truth elsewhere. At the same time, however, idolatry (frequently linked with immorality)[19] is condemned. Although there was opposition to what was seen as a denial of the truth, therefore, there was a recognition of what was seen to be true.

Second, we should perhaps remember the parable about the sheep and the goats.[20] This, we are told, concerns the judgement of the nations. The sheep are saved and the goats condemned, not on the basis of their allegiance to Christ, but because of what they have done to assist the hungry and thirsty, the stranger and the naked, the sick and the prisoner. Men and women are judged, not on the basis of their beliefs, but on whether – consciously or subconsciously – they have acted out the gospel in their lives. Those who have ministered to others have ministered to Christ himself *by being like him.*

Third, in contrast to the aggressive missionary zeal that has sometimes been seen in the Church, we find Paul setting out his approach in these terms: 'we are ambassadors for Christ . . . we entreat you on behalf of Christ, be reconciled to God' (2 Corinthians 5.20). The gospel he offers concerns Christ, who identified himself with those who were alienated from God, in order to reconcile them (2 Corinthians 5.18–19, 21). Paul then explains how he offers this gospel; it is by enduring calamities, imprisonments and hunger, by accepting dishonour and shame, by sharing suffering, poverty and death – in other words, by following in the steps of Christ, identifying himself with others.[21]

The gospel we offer is about Christ crucified. Nothing could be less aggressive than that! A few years ago, there was a frequently quoted slogan in use to the effect that 'the medium is the message'.[22] Perhaps we should adapt that a little, and suggest that our message shows us the method. Mission is rooted in holiness – in becoming like Christ, who is the image of God.

Notes

1. Genesis 1.
2. Isaiah 55.11.
3. John Wesley, 'The Large Minutes', in Thomas Jackson (ed.), *Works*, 1829–31, Vol. VIII, p. 300.
4. Sermon on the New Birth III.17.
5. 'A Plain Account of the People Called Methodists', 1748, in *Works*, ed. Thomas Jackson, 1829–31, Vol. VIII, p. 253.
6. A short discussion of the way in which the emphasis in the Methodist Church shifted from personal holiness to social holiness is found in David Clough, 'Theology through Social and Political Action', in Clive Marsh et al. (eds), *Unmasking Methodist Theology*, London: Continuum, 2004, pp. 41–7.
7. 1 Corinthians 9.19–22.
8. Galatians 4.4f.; 2 Corinthians 5.21; 8.9.
9. See further Frances Young, 'University Sermon for the Tercentenary of the Birth of John Wesley', *Epworth Review* 31 (2004), pp. 44–51.
10. See Anton Wessels, *Europe: Was it Ever Really Christian?*, ET John Bowden, London: SCM Press, 1994.
11. See above, Chapter 3.

12. 1 Corinthians 3.2.
13. See above, Chapter 2.
14. *Evening Standard*, 2 March 2010.
15. Richard Dawkins, *The God Delusion*, London: Transworld Publishers, 2006.
16. 1 Thessalonians 1.9.
17. See above, Chapter 4.
18. See Acts 17.28; 1 Corinthians 15.33; Titus 1.12.
19. For example Romans 1.23–5; 1 Corinthians 6.9–11; 2 Corinthians 6.14–18; 1 Thessalonians 1.9 and 4.3–5. Immorality is used as a symbol for idolatry in Hosea, for example 1.2; 4.10–12; 5.3–4; 9.1.
20. Matthew 25.31–46.
21. 2 Corinthians 5.21—6.10.
22. The phrase was coined by Marshall McLuhan, and used by him in his book *Understanding Media: The Extensions of Man*, Cambridge, MA: MIT Press, 1964.

Appendix

Voices in the City

ROGER COTTERRELL

The lectures on which this book is based were planned to celebrate a long history of Methodism in the West End of London. But, very importantly, beyond that they were also envisaged as a stimulus for an urgent and entirely contemporary project. The lecture programme was intended to connect with a wide-ranging review of the nature and place of Christian mission in the specific context of a busy city church (Hinde Street Methodist Church, London) with its extensive and long-established range of social work outreach projects. Beyond that, the organizers hoped to use the lectures to stimulate and provide a focus for an informal and open popular conversation about the nature of mission, and especially about the particular challenges for Christian living created by the ever-extending and ever more complex environment of the modern 'big city' – with all its problems and opportunities for those living in it.

The large audiences for these lectures were actively encouraged to participate in debate about them. After each lecture there was time for questions and comments, and the final meeting, abandoning the lecture format as such, was organized as an open audience discussion, led by the two lecturers. Though the venue was a Methodist church, Anglicans and members of other denominations attended. No doubt there were other people attracted by a strong concern with religious issues but who might well have been unsure what church 'label' to attach to themselves, or who might have wished to avoid any such defining label. The audiences included people associated with the urban social work projects of the West London Mission (as clients or workers). Some people who attended came considerable distances, from different parts of London and beyond. And there were visitors to the city, sojourners just passing through – but, as such, also part of its fluctuating population. The recorded audience comments cannot be regarded as a cross-section of views from the city. But as spontaneous responses they provide food for thought alongside the lectures.

In what follows, excerpts from those responses are set out with some linking comments offered from my 'lay' perspective as a long-time resident of London and a Methodist, with a professional background in sociology and legal and political theory but not theology. The 'voices in the city' (VIC) presented here remain anonymous since they are intended only as indicative suggestions of ways of thinking and evocations of certain kinds of experience. They are not intended to represent fully the detail and context of their authors' views (which would be impossible in the space available). They may, however, suggest *general* ideas and issues that can relate to this book's theme of urban mission while being drawn from the very personal, concrete and diverse religious experience of individuals in a particular time and place.

The nature of the city

Can the modern 'big city' be, at the same time, benighted Babylon and also the place in which the New Jerusalem might be glimpsed and worked for? The classic social theorists – Max Weber, Emile Durkheim and Karl Marx – understood that modern cities are fundamentally different in character from ancient ones. The ancient city might have seemed exceptional, unnatural; but the modern city increasingly is where almost all of us live – the normal setting of collective existence, for good or ill; a place where people escape small town communal constraints and expectations, or join and build new networks of community of many different kinds – based, for example, on business links, common projects or employment relations, family or friendship groups, shared allegiances, beliefs or values, or common neighbourhoods, languages, traditions or ethnic origins. But many urban dwellers are 'left behind', lonely, helpless and isolated.

VIC1: [to Morna Hooker]:
  You began by setting out the problems of the cities – too big and unfriendly and [for] those of us who would aspire to have even

a fraction of 150 friends – well, we're not there yet! But if that is the case, then at no point should we be struggling *for* cities, it seemed to me. If the heavenly city is the New Jerusalem, isn't it a bit daft to consider a city as a sign of heaven?

VIC2:

I was a bit disturbed by the way you began, with an extremely negative view of the city. My view of the city is very positive and I think for many people in the big city it can be a very positive view; a view that delights in the diversity of the city, the richness of variety of the people in it, and the variety of outlooks and life-styles and attitudes, and that surely carries over also to churches and faith groups. You ask how the Church can tackle the forces of injustice in the city, and that seems a strange question to me because in London, for example, there are many different churches, many different people trying to find ways of translating the gospel into action, and people of other faiths who are trying to translate *their* gospel into action. I wonder whether the solution to the problems is not to say how 'we' should do things; it's simply to try to recognize an infinity of ways of exploring the richness of material life and spiritual life in the city.

VIC3:

I'm a lay worker and part of my job is visiting people. I do find that there are people who are left behind and especially the elderly. In the old days you could turn up at somebody's door and say, 'I'm from the church and I'm visiting you.' Now you have to make an appointment. If they don't know you're coming they're startled. 'Oh, you *know I'm still here*! You're *visiting* me. Oh, come in.' My neighbour, who used to receive my post when I was at work, died and I didn't even know. Three weeks later her flat was being cleared. So what is our responsibility? How do we look out for our neighbours in this big city that we live in?

VIC4:

I come originally from a village in Dorset. I knew every single person in that village. I left school at 15 and since then all of my life has been lived in cities. That village . . . like you say, maybe it was idyllic, but when I lived there the thatched cottages were almost fallen in ruins. No one wanted to know about them; now they're all done up, worth half a million or whatever. And that village, it's like a ghost town, all the doors are shut; the garages and doors are locked shut. No village shops. It's just people coming from London for Saturday and Sunday. The local people born there have gone years ago. In the city you do have a chance; there are advantages in different ways of living. The problems of the city get overcome as time goes by.

The city is surely not just 'two cities' – rich and poor; winners and losers – though it harbours scandalous disparities of wealth. It may also be a place where people become rich or poor in many different ways. Some relative 'losers' in material terms become rich in ways they define for themselves and that are rooted in their own communal networks; and 'winners' may be spiritually poor in ways they hardly recognize as they are carried along by the city's frenetic pace of activity, fads and fashions, transient projects, temptations and distractions.

Church and mission

Presumably no one form of Church may be fully appropriate given the immense variety of urban life. That variety, however, makes many social networks fluid and fluctuating. Is it possible to think of Christian mission as a single idea in this context, or must we treat the whole idea of mission as shaped by very diverse expectations about what Church is or could be?

VIC5:
Anything that's called 'Church' today is not the Church. The Church is characterized by the way that Jesus lived with his friends and also by the way the friends lived together after he had gone away. But they eventually became invisible and went underground, and the name 'Church' was taken over by institution and organization, and has been ever since. My Church for today is friends that I live with.

VIC6:
I've been to services, and there have been builders come across from sites to take communion. There's another church near here

[where] there are people who haven't much; they were talking about a guy who had come in who was homeless and had never been to church before and he said after four weeks of coming, well he came because the people loved him. I thought that was brilliant. It's very easy to be in any church and just have people like you or like me, and the people who are different find it difficult to join in. We have a lot of different churches now. . . . Maybe we'll be having little cells where people of the same sort of understanding meet together and we accept each other. That may be the future.

Learning about Christianity

The 'same sort of understanding' – but what sort of understanding of Christian doctrine is necessary? The following two views mark out contrasting terrain – on the one hand perhaps linking to comments in this book on traditional practices and institutions by which Christian knowledge has been passed on; on the other suggesting that the task of conveying understanding needs much rethinking in the light of current scepticisms.

VIC7:
> Our two children grew up in the Methodist Church through Sunday School and have grown up to be socially responsible, environmentally aware people, but as soon as they were old enough they stopped going to church. They have no problems with Jesus. The problems they have are with God. I grew up at a time when *Honest to God* was coming about and that was my lifeline and it seems to me that in the world of Richard Dawkins, unless we can articulate what it is that we fundamentally *mean* by God, rather than just saying 'God this . . .' and 'God that . . .', we might as well forget religion as we know it. But all the things that Jesus stands for, lots of people are doing and they don't relate to God at all.

VIC8:
> I grew up in Africa. My grandmother was a Methodist and when I came here I attended a [Methodist] college. The thing that I learned from my principal, Dr Skevington Wood, is that to grow

in this church you have to learn to understand the function of the Church. And all we need is a hymn book and the Bible. He used to tell me that when he was young all he did was get into the church, open the book, Wesley's hymns – and that was the theology that we have to get into ourselves. That's what I normally do when I come in here. I open the book, look at the hymn board and read the hymns. I'm getting more out of this church than I can any other way. And I thank God for that.

Cultural and religious pluralism

Big cities, by their nature, *have to* celebrate diversity. They are places of continuous change (in populations, built environment, social and cultural life, economic activity) where new ideas develop quickly and are tested out in living; where strangers *must* meet, interact and co-operate; where social networks are real but very varied in character, some much stronger and more enduring than others. The key issue is how to *communicate*, how to reach out – in Christian terms how to love the stranger as a neighbour whose similarity to (but also difference from) 'us' is acknowledged, respected and welcomed. What seems to be required is a continuous effort of understanding – but one that does not demand a promise of future, unquestioning conformity to 'our' ways as a pre-condition for that effort to be made.

VIC9:

> I work in Belmarsh Prison as a volunteer in the visits hall and I meet a lot of people who are Muslims. I did a distance-learning theology degree a while ago and a module on Islam so I informed myself a bit. The surprise on people's faces when you say to them, 'Are you a Muslim?' They look suspicious. But you ask them about Eid or Ramadan, and immediately you get a response – relief that you are not criticizing them, you're empathizing with them. That's where you can start – finding out about what they do believe and sharing the things that are positive. Because we do worship one God, and we have things like Abraham and Noah in common. Start where you have something in common and then you gain confidence.

VIC10:

I am an Anglican married to a Roman Catholic. The conclusion we reached was that we would not allow the churches to divide our families. We go to both churches alternately, and are well received into both. Getting to know an American who lived in London opened up to me a whole new society, threaded through London life, of expatriates. They have, on the whole, generated their own social groups who come from lots of different countries and who in a way operate within our society but separate from our society. Many will hardly know a British person or will rarely have been into a British person's home. So I wanted to try to introduce into this fascinating discussion [some] thought about 'witness', which probably, being British, I find a bit easier than 'proselytizing' or 'conversion'. I think it [would be] a reasonable objective, in this multi-ethnic, multi-background London society, if you could accept some of these people from other countries into your life and maybe into your home and you might manage to do a bit of witness which said: 'I'm a Christian and this is how I behave; I'm probably too shy to explain, unless you really ask what I mean by all that, but I will *demonstrate*, by what I am and how I behave and how I talk about things, that I am a Christian.' Maybe that's how I would define witness, and that's about as much as I could manage, but it's more than I do at the moment. And, from the evidence I see, it's more than a lot of Christians do in London already. To somehow put your arms around some of the people who have come to join our society and to show them what being a Christian is, whatever variety of Christian you are.

VIC11:

I wonder whether part of the challenge of the biblical revelation about the city is the picture of us all together – different languages, tribes, nations. The city throws us together in a way that forces us to ask whether we are for ourselves and our friendship groups and we are going to limit ourselves to those who are like us, or whether we actually listen to the revelation of God of inclusion. We're forced together; we see the vast differences, and part of the biblical challenge is how we are going to respond.

Power, conformity and unity

The material presented in Chapter 4 provoked much post-lecture discussion about relationships between Christianity and political power, and about issues of power and hierarchy in the Church itself. Was Constantine, finally, really a Christian? Can 'Christian' be defined in a way that accepts coercive power alongside love of God and neighbour? This issue, as discussed in earlier pages of this book, touches on many aspects of the organization of the Church and the possibilities of Church unity and ecumenism, as well as the responsibilities of Christians to challenge hierarchies and structures of authority in pursuit of a kingdom of God free of any image of earthly kingship. But it touches also on many very local issues of power – in the way particular church congregations operate, and the equal respect due to their members.

VIC12:

If a fundamental element in Constantine's policy was to establish unity, could he be seen as the first ecumenist? If so, in the light of the experience of the bishoprics in the succeeding generations and perhaps our understanding that power corrupts and ultimate power corrupts ultimately, I wonder what lessons we might learn and what dangers we should heed in our current thinking of unity within the life of the Church.

VIC13:

I've been told that before Roman Catholicism came into this country there was the Celtic movement; women had a much more important part, there was much more emphasis on the supernatural and it was a more bottom-up approach. I would love to see something more along those lines. I have been in house churches in the distant past. When I was about 20, they seemed to be about the only way things could go. Now I'm 60 I don't see it quite that way but I would hate it if there was going to be something very authoritarian and very top-down – [where] you either belong or you're not a Christian.

VIC14:

I come from a fairly evangelical stable . . . There are a lot of women I know, about my age, I'm 61, and they were and still are fervent Christians but they do not go to any church regularly. They are single, well educated; they manage their own finance, they don't have a man dictating to them, and in their jobs they have to use their minds, often dealing with finance. They go to church: *nobody* cares what they think and their opinions are just not sought. Educated women have not been allowed to use their God-given skills in the Church. A friend of mine was told off for providing the wrong sort of biscuits! She is educated enough and knows the Bible well enough to have people in her home for Bible study but she isn't supposed to have the sort of intelligence that can decide what sort of biscuits to have.

Practical mission

Surely the two models of mission – evangelistic and practical – discussed in this book are indeed inseparable. But in the city, can one 'be holy as I am holy' partly by quietly playing one's individual part alongside others, contributing conscientiously to what Durkheim described as the networks of social solidarity on which complex modern society relies? Positive, deliberate outreach often seems difficult in a city of strangers where one must work within many complex and intricate social networks. But the city can sometimes appear (not quite paradoxically) as a mosaic of 'villages' in which people may act locally for each other and with each other. It can be a place of political action at many levels. It can also be a place of interpersonal concern that shows itself in small but significant acts whose effects ripple through urban structures that may otherwise seem too monolithic for any single person to hope to change.

VIC15:
We run a day centre for elderly people in our church building and use a lot of volunteers. One really big problem where I live is people who are long-term unemployed. [There are] enormous hurdles [for them] getting back to work but we have had a brilliant success: our driver came to us having had ten years of terrible mental health. We've nurtured him and he's done a wonderful job driving our minibus and just got a job. Of course we are thrilled, but it leaves us without a bus driver. We have about

40 volunteers working for us. Not all are going to be a success like that but we are providing a nurturing opportunity for them where they can recover or look for opportunities. We had a man last year who went to work for McDonald's and has been working there for a whole year. We're thrilled with those successes.

VIC16:

I'm a trustee of a charity called London Citizens and we proposed a living wage for London. What we have been doing is going into the boardrooms and basically asking the chairmen of places like banks and hospitals to repent! [audience laughter]. We say, 'Why are you paying your cleaners a wage on which they cannot live in London, and will you not consider paying a London living wage?' At the moment, that's £7.60 an hour, compared with roughly £2 below that – the national minimum wage – which is what a lot of employers try to get away with. Churches and other faith groups, and other people of good will, together can raise questions and also provide models of what could be done. The living wage isn't a legal requirement, but it's a moral benchmark to which you can appeal to people to say: if you want to raise children and families out of poverty, pay them a decent wage.

VIC17:

Some people would say London isn't a city at all, just a collection of villages which happen to adjoin each other. What's often true is that it's community action at the local level that makes the difference to the quality of life in that particular area. Certainly, some decades ago, Covent Garden was saved from the property developers by concerted community development action, and I'm sure there are more recent examples. So we shouldn't necessarily see the city as this shapeless thing that can only be controlled by government or by control from above. I think resistance and change from below is also an important part of being a citizen.

VIC18 [responding to the above]

There are issues there, though, about where power is and what capacity people have to act, because of education and resources; so different parts of the city have different capacities.

As these extracts illustrate, the contributions of those who discussed the lectures were very varied. The speakers included ministers of religion, churchgoers of various denominations, people who have suffered serious misfortune in their lives and sought help in the churches, people who love city life, others who tolerate it, must reconcile themselves to it, or are seeking to improve it, and yet others who have personal experience of its darker aspects. Taken together, their statements perhaps give some indication of the wide range of interest which Morna Hooker's and Frances Young's lectures provoked, and of some popular issues which surely deserve to be addressed in contemporary debates on urban mission.

Index of Subjects and Names

Index of Scriptural References